Cambridge Elements ☰

Elements in Quantitative and Computational Methods
for the Social Sciences
edited by
R. Michael Alvarez
California Institute of Technology
Nathaniel Beck
New York University

T0286843

AGENT-BASED MODELS OF POLARIZATION AND ETHNOCENTRISM

Michael Laver

New York University

CAMBRIDGE
UNIVERSITY PRESS

CAMBRIDGE
UNIVERSITY PRESS

University Printing House, Cambridge CB2 8BS, United Kingdom

One Liberty Plaza, 20th Floor, New York, NY 10006, USA

477 Williamstown Road, Port Melbourne, VIC 3207, Australia

314–321, 3rd Floor, Plot 3, Splendor Forum, Jasola District Centre,
New Delhi – 110025, India

79 Anson Road, #06–04/06, Singapore 079906

Cambridge University Press is part of the University of Cambridge.

It furthers the University's mission by disseminating knowledge in the pursuit of
education, learning, and research at the highest international levels of excellence.

www.cambridge.org
Information on this title: www.cambridge.org/9781108796408
DOI: 10.1017/9781108854788

First published 2020

A catalogue record for this publication is available from the British Library.

ISBN 978-1-108-79640-8 Paperback
ISSN 2398-4023 (online)
ISSN 2514-3794 (print)

Additional resources for this publication at www.cambridge.org/laver2.

Agent-Based Models of Polarization and Ethnocentrism

Elements in Quantitative and Computational Methods for the Social Sciences

DOI: 10.1017/9781108854788
First published online: March 2020

Michael Laver
New York University
Author for correspondence: ml127@nyu.edu

Abstract: Building on the Cambridge Element *Agent-Based Models of Social Life: Fundamentals* (Cambridge, 2020), we move on to the next level. We do this by building agent-based models of polarization and ethnocentrism. In the process we develop the following: stochastic models, which add a crucial element of uncertainty to human interaction; models of human interactions structured by social networks; and evolutionary models in which agents using more effective decision rules are more likely to survive and prosper than others. The aim is to leave readers with an effective toolkit for building, running, and analyzing agent-based models of social interaction.

Keywords: agent-based models, social interaction, polarization, ethnocentrism, simulation

ISBNs: 9781108796408 (PB), 9781108854788 (OC)
ISSNs: 2398-4023 (online), 2514-3794 (print)

Contents

Code files for all named NetLogo models (set in bold text) referred to in this Element are available at www.cambridge.org/laver2.

1 Introduction

In the first Element in this pair, *Agent-Based Models of Social Life: Fundamentals*, we got up and running with agent-based modeling (ABM) and then exercised our mental muscles by torturing the classic Schelling segregation model. If you've done no agent-based modeling before and/or are not familiar with the NetLogo ABM platform, then you should read the first Element, which introduces you to these things, before going any further. I devote this Element to different examples of social interaction, each offering different types of insight and posing different modeling challenges. This lets us develop models that are more powerful. We now use our new computational tools to dig deeper into how ABMs can help us explore implications of various theories of social interaction. Code files for all named NetLogo models (set in bold text) referred to in this Element are available at www.cambridge.org/laver2.

Following the precedent set in the first Element of sticking with one model and really pulling it to pieces, Sections 2, 3, and 4 focus on the evolution of public opinion, and in particular the evolution of *polarized* public opinion. We begin in Section 2 with a simple model of social interaction, each interaction causing tiny random, but slightly biased, shifts in individual agents' opinions. We sort people into social groups, assuming they're more likely to interact socially with members of their own group than with members of another group. Indeed, one way of thinking of a social group is as a collection of people more likely to interact with each other than with outsiders. We introduce those hardliners we all know, people who love to broadcast their own opinions but never listen to anyone else. The model we create using these basic building blocks gives us simple but powerful intuitions about the evolution of polarization in public attitudes. The model's code is very simple, and the big theoretical insight from Section 2 is that we can now model agents' preferences not as something fixed in advance by the omniscient theorist, but as evolving endogenously and possibly in unexpected ways during the process of social interaction.

Most social interactions are *not* completely random, and it is now common to describe these in terms of social networks. We do this in Section 3. NetLogo has a powerful "Network" extension, which allows you to create new agents who are located on one of several different types of social network, and we exploit this capability. We put agents from two different social groups, including each groups' hardliners, on two different social networks, allow limited social connections between the two groups, and restrict social interactions that affect people's opinions to those between network neighbors rather than between any random pair of people in the same group. We compare two very different social network structures, though NetLogo offers you the possibility of investigating several others. The first are random networks, which generate patterns of social interaction quite like those in the baseline random interaction model we set up in Section 2. We also investigate preferential attachment networks, said to resemble real social networks we find "in the wild," for example, in social media. We find striking differences between the evolution of public opinion on these very different types of social network, with highly connected agents in preferential attachment networks counteracting the effects of hardliners on polarization. Methodologically, this section introduces you to the design and coding of network-based models of social interaction, which are both increasingly common and quite difficult to analyze in systematic ways other than with computer simulations. Theoretically, results in this section provide striking examples of how network structure can make a big difference when modeling social interaction.

Section 4 looks at the evolution of public opinion when people belong to *overlapping* social groups, which may pull them in different directions. These groups may arise from any cleavage in society such that, as noted above, people tend to interact with others from the same group and not with people from other groups. We might be talking about age, occupation, religion, or indeed anything else that has an effect in the real world on the structure of social interaction. In Sections 2 and 3 we investigated the effect of just one social cleavage such as this. Things get more complicated if there is more than one cleavage. Say one cleavage divides people into ups and downs, while another divides people into lefts and rights. It now makes a big difference to social interaction, for example, if all the ups are also lefts or if half of the ups are lefts and half are rights. In the latter case, the evolution of public opinion is affected by the fact that the ups are now cross-pressured by their two group memberships. In the former case they are not. While this is now quite a rich and complex model of the endogenous evolution of public opinion, it's still easy to program and tease out its implications by extending our NetLogo model of social interaction.

We turn in Section 5 to a different topic, captured by an influential model of "rational ethnocentrism" proposed by Hammond and Axelrod.[1] Agents are once more sorted into groups and then play Prisoners' Dilemma (PD) games with their neighbors. (We'll explain the PD game when we come to it.) An important feature of this model is that it takes us much further than we've gone before into a world that is evolutionary, where the more successful agents reproduce with a higher probability than others. The influential published finding of this model is that "ethnocentric" agents – those who cooperate with others from of their own group but defect against people from other groups – tend to prosper relative

---

[1] Hammond, R. A. and R. Axelrod (2006). The evolution of ethnocentrism. *Journal of Conflict Resolution* **50**: 926–36.

to rivals who do not condition their behavior on the ethnicity of the person they are dealing with. The key claim, therefore, is that "ethnocentrism pays." A faithful rendition of the Hammond-Axelrod model is also in the NetLogo models library. This allows us to replicate published results but also allows us to see that these results are very fragile, falling apart in the face of small but plausible changes in modeling assumptions. For example, we can use this model to generate "ethnocentric" behavior even when all agents belong to the same ethnic group, which makes no sense whatsoever.

Having shown this, we move on to modify and extend the model in ways that allow you to develop a better understanding of settings in which we observe behavior that might reasonably be described as "ethnocentric." Among the more interesting findings is that, if we accept what turns out to be the very restrictive definition of ethnocentrism in the baseline model, then we can create settings in which *a dominant population of ethnocentric agents can evolve from settings in which there are no ethnocentric agents at all*!

Even if your main interest is in something other than ethnocentrism, however, this section introduces you to a simple but powerful evolutionary approach to modeling that you can use in many other contexts. Indeed, the main point of this whole Element is not to talk about ethnocentrism or the evolution of public opinion per se, though these are interesting topics in themselves. My aim is to give you a good sense of the many different ways in which you can deploy agent-based modeling to explore any social interaction that fascinates you.

2 Polarization of Public Opinion

Where do our preferences, tastes, and opinions come from? The short answer is that we're not born with them; they evolve from our interactions with other people. Back in 1951 Solomon Asch[2] reported results of a now-famous psychological experiment in a paper with a title that says it all: "Effects of group pressure upon the modification and distortion of judgment."

Asch put experimental subjects in a group with others they thought were fellow subjects but who were in fact stooges. For each trial of the experiment, Asch showed members of the group a line on a card, asking them to match its length with one of three other lines. One of the other lines was the same length; the other two were clearly different lengths. Group members announced their answers in turn, with the experimental subject coming last. The experiment was run 18 times with lines of different lengths. In the control group, stooges were primed to give the correct answer every time, always matching the lines of the

---

[2] Asch, S. E. (1951). Effects of group pressure upon the modification and distortion of judgment. In H. Guetzkow (ed.), *Groups, leadership and men*. Pittsburgh, PA: Carnegie Press.

same length. In the treatment group, the stooges were primed to start by giving correct answers on the first few trials, then suddenly to switch to giving obviously wrong answers for many of the subsequent trials, though sometimes giving a correct answer.

The results were striking. In control groups, where stooges always gave the correct answer, subjects almost never made a mistake about the length of the line. In treatment groups, where experimental subjects' own two eyes clearly said one thing and the rest of the group said something quite different, subjects often gave a wrong answer that conformed with that of the group. Comparing a short line with a long and a short line, if the group said the short line was long, then the subjects often also said the short line was long, even when they could clearly see this was not true. This is an example of something we can think of as group conformity. Subsequent generations of social psychological research have confirmed and refined this conclusion.

Something similar is likely going on with us when we evolve our own preferences, tastes, and opinions. I probably speak for many when I say that I have opinions about genetically modified organisms, global warming, and *in vitro* fertilization. I expect I'm also like many in having these opinions despite, if I'm honest, knowing next to nothing about these matters, particularly about the science involved in each of them. So how do I develop firm preferences, tastes, and opinions on matters about which I am so ignorant? There are several answers to this question, but the answer I consider here has to do with social interaction. My opinions don't pop out of thin air or lurk in my DNA but emerge endogenously as a product of my interactions with others. We'll soon see that, if two otherwise identical people interact with different social groups, then their opinions tend to evolve from the same starting point to be different from each other, sometimes strikingly different.

We start by modeling the evolution of private preferences in a social world characterized by more-or-less random interactions between pairs of individuals. In each interaction, a random one of the pair is speaker and the other listener. These interactions are repeated many times, so everyone will frequently be either speaker or listener.

Each interaction changes the listener's views a little, and each change has two components. The first component is *reaction* and is essentially random. The listener's views might change in any direction following the interaction – possibly moving toward, possibly away from the views of the speaker. The idea here is that, if I say something to you, there's a lot of uncertainty about how you react to this. You may hate what I say, so your opinion evolves away from mine. You may love what I say, so your opinion evolves toward mine. Or you may be indifferent, in which case what I say has no systematic effect on you.

The second component of the change in the listener's views is *attraction* and leverages what we know about the general tendencies toward social conformity we just discussed. This generates a slight tendency, other things being equal, for the listener's views to move toward those expressed by the speaker.

If the assumption of even a modicum of social attraction worries you, think about what would happen if the reverse were true, if, other things being equal, social interactions tended systematically to make people's views diverge. Social interaction would then tend to result in repulsion rather than attraction. This would create what would look like an exploding universe of public opinion, with everyone's opinions becoming ever more diverse and different from each other. The possibility of people ever agreeing on anything would become increasingly remote. As we will see, the reaction component of an interaction will often actually move the listener's view *away* from the speaker much more than the attraction component moves it *toward* the speaker. On average in large populations over long periods, when two people interact in our model, the combination of random reaction with some small attraction toward the speaker is somewhat more likely to move their views together than apart.

We need to do one more thing before we roll up our sleeves and start building the model. This is to describe people's opinions systematically. We summarize opinions in a way you've probably been using most of your life, whether or not you realize it. Think about what we mean when we say that someone is to the right or the left, or at the center, of the political spectrum. We're summarizing people's opinions *as if* they could be described in terms of a line, or dimension, that runs from left to right. If I say that "Jack's opinions are way to the right of mine" or "Jill's opinions are way to the left," you pretty much understand what I mean. You don't reply, "I've no idea what you're talking about." People have opinions on many different things, but their opinions on different things tend to be correlated. So when I tell you that Jack favors open carry gun laws, banning all abortions, and deporting all immigrants, then I probably won't have to tell you where he stands on gay marriage. You could guess wrongly, but you would probably guess correctly because people's opinions on this bundle of issues tend to be correlated. This means we can describe these opinions as if they can all be summarized in terms of a single underlying policy dimension, which in this case we might think of as liberal versus conservative.

This lies behind a widespread convention within the social sciences of describing people's opinions and preferences using policy spaces spanned by a small number of dimensions – left-right, liberal-conservative, hawk-dove, and so on. For our models of the evolution of public opinion, therefore, we're going to interpret the NetLogo model world not as a physical space but as a two-dimensional opinion space that we can use to describe the preferences, tastes,

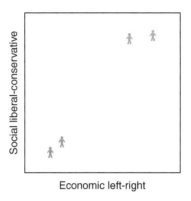

Figure 2.1 Agent preferences in a two-dimensional policy space

and opinions of all agents. Figure 2.1 shows an example of this. I labeled the horizontal dimension as summarizing "left vs. right" positions on economic policy and the vertical dimension as summarizing "liberal vs. conservative" positions on social and moral policy. But you may think of completely different dimensions on which people's opinions and attitudes differ systematically, in which case feel free to substitute your own ideas. What is important is that there are systematic ways to describe the differences of opinion we find in any human population.

There are two pink agents in the bottom left of the preference space shown in Figure 2.1. Betraying my European origins, I will tell you that these are leftist on economic policy and liberal on social policy. The two blue agents in the top right of the space are rightist on economic policy and conservative on social policy. But we can imagine people who have preferences that put them at any point in the space. In the bottom right we might have libertarians on the economic right because they favor drastically reducing the role of the state in the economy, but also very liberal because they also favor reducing the role of the state in matters of individual morality. In the top left we might find radical nationalists who favor left-wing economic policies but also traditional social values.

The Model: Roadmap

We use the term social group to describe a collection of people who are much more likely to interact with people from the same group than with others. Members of each group therefore share some characteristic, possibly hidden even to themselves, that structures their social interactions. Examples might be age, occupation, hobby, gender, religion, and language. What such characteristics might be and how we might label any given social group are completely beside the point for the arguments I will make in what follows – they might be chess players, Star Trek fans, or whatever. People who belong to the social groups that concern us are more likely to interact socially with others from the same group than with people from others.

We begin with a simple model of social interaction in which everyone belongs to the same social group. We initialize the dynamics of public opinion by scattering everyone's opinions at random in the type of opinion space shown in Figure 2.1. In each iteration of the model, each agent randomly chooses a peer with whom to interact. The calling agent is listener in this interaction, the peer is speaker. After every interaction between a pair of agents, the opinions of the listener shift a little, according to the twin factors of reaction and attraction sketched earlier and precisely described in what follows. This process of social interaction continues forever or until we stop the simulation. What we observe in every model run is steady evolution from the initial random scatter of opinions all over the map to a coherent bell-shaped distribution of these opinions.

We'll get to the model soon, but Figure 2.2 shows what the evolved distribution of public opinion generated by our model typically looks like. The top panel shows an evolved distribution of 1,000 agents' opinions, which were first scattered at random all over the model world, after many iterations of the model. The bottom panel plots the evolved distribution of these opinions on the horizontal axis, showing that this is indeed the bell-shaped normal distribution, or something very close to it, that characterizes many natural phenomena that evolve on the basis of random processes.

Every time you run this simple model of social interaction with the same parameters, a similar bell-shaped distribution of preferences will evolve. Every time, however, the center of this distribution will be different. (Sometimes, annoyingly, the bell shape will be hard to see because it wraps around the edges of the NetLogo world!) These differences arise because, at some point after the model iterates many times, a little random cluster of agents forms around some location in the opinion space. This cluster then acts like a piece of grit around which a pearl forms in an oyster – as a center of mass that attracts other agents, who attract still more agents, and so on. This initial random cluster acts as an attractor in the dynamic system we have set up. The precise location of this initial cluster, however, is random. The amount of variation in agents' opinions within this distribution, as we will see, is a function of the model parameters specifying the level of reaction and attraction in these interactions.

The idea that the locations of the centers of these distributions of public opinion are completely random may seem peculiar. We address this with an extension to the model introducing a new species of agent – the hardliner. Hardliners are those people we have all (sadly) met who speak a lot but never

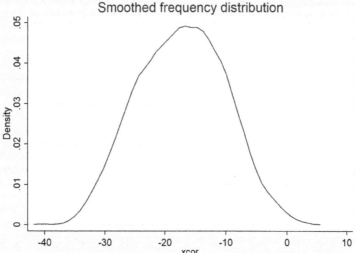

Figure 2.2 Evolved bell-shaped distribution of public opinion

listen. When hardliners interact with peers, therefore, they *never* change their own opinions. If we create a small cohort of hardliners (say just 2 percent of the population) and scatter their opinions around some particular point in the space, then they act as anchors in the evolution of the opinions of the entire rest of the population. The bell-shaped distribution that evolves is then always centered on the opinions of the hardliners.

We see this in Figure 2.3, which shows an evolved bell-shaped distribution of 1,000 agents' opinions. This distribution is centered on the opinions of just 10 hardliners who, throughout thousands of cycles of interaction, never budged from their starting locations in the upper right quadrant of the opinion space. The hardliners are the little gray men in this figure, other agents are blue. Given

Figure 2.3 Evolved bell-shaped distribution of public opinion; one social group and 1 percent (gray) hardliners

just a few hardliners at this location, they eventually drag the opinions of all other group members toward them, just as a few donkeys can (albeit slowly) pull a huge battleship in a friction-free world. The evolution of public opinion is now almost identical every time we run the model.

We're mainly interested in social processes that might underlie *polarization* of public opinion. We can think of polarization in terms of distributions of agents' opinions that are bimodal or even multimodal, with the modes (peaks) of the distribution being relatively far apart from each other. We can easily use our model to generate such distributions if we have more than one social group, recalling that members of each group are more likely to interact socially with others from their own group than with members of a different group.

We therefore extend the model by dividing our population into two social groups. You can have more groups than two if you prefer (feel free to experiment with this), but key intuitions from the model arrive once there are two groups. We quickly see that this generates a dynamics of social interaction in which members of different groups evolve to have different distributions of opinion. Sometimes these distributions are very different from each other, so that public opinion as a whole evolves to be polarized.

Figure 2.4 shows an evolved bimodal and polarized distribution of public opinion in a setting with two equal-sized social groups. Each group has 2 percent hardliners, with the opinions of the hardliners in each group having distinctive locations in the opinion space. To make the point, this is the output of a run of the model with the extreme setting that agents interact *only* with members of their own group and never with members of the other group. As we will see, allowing some intergroup interaction substantially reduces polarization.

Figure 2.4 Evolved bimodal distribution of public opinion; two social groups and 2 percent (gray) hardliners

A Model of Endogenous Preference Evolution: NetLogo Code

This is a model I wrote my own self, and it is not in the NetLogo models library. As with the Schelling segregation model, however, NetLogo code for this model of the endogenous evolution of public opinion is simple and easy to read. The baseline model is **Evolution of preferences 1.0**.

Setup and Housekeeping

There are two breeds of agent in this model, citizens and hardliners:

```
breed [citizens citizen]
breed [hardliners hardliner]
```

Use breeds of agent in NetLogo whenever you want to instruct different types of agent to do different things. Here, you can now ask just the hardliners to do something, or just the citizens. This is a useful feature of NetLogo, though you must always provide, first, the plural and then the singular name of the breed. NetLogo still addresses all agents, regardless of breed, as `turtles`. If this irritates you, and it does irritate certain people of a febrile disposition, you can define a new breed `[people person]`, set all agents' breed to people as soon as you create them, and then ask people instead of turtles to do things. I myself am an easygoing person, however, and don't mind working with turtles.

A single global variable, n-pop, is declared in the body of the code. This records the total number of people in the population. We will declare other globals on the interface.

Agents belong to one of two groups, colored pink and blue, recorded in the agent variable group. Agents store the identity of their current peer in the agent variable peer. Thus:

```
turtles-own
  [
  group          ; blue or pink group?
  peer           ; "who" of agent selected for interaction
  ]
```

The setup procedure first creates two groups of agent: a total of n-pinks pink agents, and n-blues blue agents. Global variables specifying n-pinks and n-blues are set by sliders on the interface, while n-pop is the total number of agents. Once created, agents' opinions are scattered randomly throughout the NetLogo world (opinion space). All of this gives us:

```
to setup
  clear-all
  create-citizens n-pinks [set group pink set color pink]
  create-citizens n-blues [set group blue set color sky]
  set n-pop n-pinks + n-blues
  ask turtles [setxy random-xcor random-ycor]
  ...
```

Next, we turn into hardliners a small proportion (prop-hard, a global variable set by a slider on the interface) of randomly selected agents from each group.

```
...
ask n-of int(prop-hard * n-pinks) citizens with [group = pink]
    [set breed hardliners]
ask n-of int(prop-hard * n-blues) citizens with [group = blue]
    [set breed hardliners]
...
```

We now rescatter hardliners' preferences in a biased way. That is, we randomly scatter opinions of blue hardliners to have a normal distribution with a standard deviation of hard-scatter and a mean biased away from the center of the NetLogo world by a number of cells, hard-bias, to the *east and north* of center. The globals hard-bias and hard-scatter are set by sliders on the interface. Similarly, opinions of pink hardliners have a normal distribution with a standard deviation of hard-scatter and a mean biased away from the center by hard-bias cells to the *west and south* of center. We specify this biased scattering of hardliners' opinions in a separate procedure biased-scatter. We also ask hardliners to double their size, take the shape of a person, and color themselves gray when shown on the interface. We ask patches to color themselves white. All of this gives us:

```
...
ask hardliners
    [biased-scatter set shape "person" set size 2 set color gray]
ask patches [set pcolor white]
reset-ticks
end

to biased-scatter
   ifelse group = blue
      [setxy random-normal hard-bias hard-scatter
             random-normal hard-bias hard-scatter]

      [setxy random-normal (-1 * hard-bias) hard-scatter
             random-normal (-1 * hard-bias) hard-scatter]
end
```

Social Interaction

Now that we've populated our artificial society with citizens and hardliners, the social interactions that drive the evolution of their opinions are very simple yet, as we'll see, remarkably powerful. The logical engine of the model is in the following NetLogo code:

```
to go
   ask citizens [
     set peer one-of other turtles
     ifelse [group] of peer = [group] of self
         [interact]
         [if random-float 1 < out-group-openness [interact]]]
     tick
end

to interact
   set heading random-float 360
   forward reaction
   face peer
   forward distance peer * attraction
end
```

The go procedure, which controls social interaction in the NetLogo world, first asks every citizen (not hardliners, who never change their opinions) to randomly pick a peer. The peer can be a citizen or a hardliner (set peer one-of other turtles); indeed it's crucial that the peer is sometimes a hardliner. What each agent does depends on whether the peer is from the same social group. Two different possible actions follow the conditional instruction ifelse [group] of peer = [group] of self. If the peer is from the same social group, then the agent performs the first action listed: [interact]. What it means to interact is specified in the procedure following the go procedure. Else, the peer is from a different social group; the agent then performs the second action listed, which in turn depends on another global parameter set on the interface, `out-group-openness`. This specifies the probability, which can be zero, that an agent interacts with a peer from another group. Thus: `[if random-float 1 < out-group-openness [interact]]`. This code makes agents interact with peers of other groups with probability `out-group-openness`. All that remains is to specify what it means to `interact` with a `peer`. As we discussed above, the social interaction we model has two independent components. The first component is a random reaction; the listening agent's opinions can change randomly in any direction. The second component is a systematic attraction; this causes a listening agent to shift its opinions somewhat toward its peer. The relative size of these two components is set by two global variables on the interface: `reaction` and `attraction`.

The first part of the `interact` procedure deals with the random reaction, telling agents first to face a random direction (`set heading random-float 360`), then move `forward` a number (`reaction`) of units in the NetLogo coordinate system (`forward reaction`). If `reaction` is set to 5, for example, the agent moves 5 units in a random direction. From this new location, agents turn to face their `peer` (`face peer`) then move `forward` a proportion (`attraction`) of the `distance` from their `peer` (`forward distance peer * attraction`). If `attraction` is 0.05, for example, agents move toward their peers by an amount that is 5 percent of the distance between them and the peer. The relative sizes of `reaction` and `attraction` determine how likely interacting agents are to move toward their peers. But, logically, as long as `attraction` is greater than zero, there is some positive probability of this happening.

While the model is running, it simply iterates this `interact` procedure over and over again. The result we observe is a steady evolution, from a random start, of very well defined distributions of public opinion. These distributions are more-or-less polarized, according to model parameters that we vary systematically in the following section. Since this model is not in the NetLogo models library, its full code is at the end of this section.

We've one more job to do. This is to specify what we mean by polarization of public opinion – the social phenomenon that motivates this entire exercise. There are many different ways to do this, but a simple and intuitive way is to specify two points as respective centers of each groups' distribution of opinions. We find these centers by computing the average location on each axis of the members of each group. We then define a measure of the polarization of opinion between the groups as the distance between these two group centers. We do this by defining a NetLogo reporter, `polarization`:

```
to-report polarization
  let px mean [xcor] of turtles with [group = pink]
  let bx mean [xcor] of turtles with [group = blue]
  let py mean [ycor] of turtles with [group = pink]
  let by mean [ycor] of turtles with [group = blue]
  report sqrt ((px - bx) ^ 2 + (py - by) ^ 2)
end
```

This first specifies four `let` instructions to calculate the average x and y coordinates of members of the pink and blue groups. (These `let` instructions really simplify what is going on and help avoid a big, ugly expression.) We then use Pythagoras' theorem to `report` the distance between the two group centers.

Since hardliners' opinions are randomly scattered around distinctive locations in the opinion space and never change, the polarization of their opinions will be a big factor in the polarization of others in their respective groups. We measure polarization of hardliners' opinions using a directly analogous reporter, `hard-polar`:

```
to-report hard-polar
  let hpx mean [xcor] of hardliners with [group = pink]
  let hpy mean [ycor] of hardliners with [group = pink]
  let hbx mean [xcor] of hardliners with [group = blue]
  let hby mean [ycor] of hardliners with [group = blue]
  report sqrt ((hpx - hbx) ^ 2 + (hpy - hby) ^ 2)
end
```

Different random scatters of hardliners' opinions, even with the same mean and standard deviation, will generate slightly different levels of polarization in these opinions. We want to measure the evolved polarization of public opinion relative to the polarization of hardliners. We therefore define a measure of net polarization, `net-polar`, as the level of polarization in the population, relative to the level of polarization of hardliners:

```
to-report net-polar
  report polarization / hard-polar
end
```

This measure has the nice property that, when hardliners have zero effect on the polarization of public opinion, `net-polar` will be 0. When opinions of ordinary citizens are exactly as polarized as those of their own groups' hardliners, `net-polar` will be 1.

What Affects the Polarization of Public Opinion?

We're ready to design computational experiments exploring the effect of key model parameters on evolved distributions of public opinion. While there are several of these parameters, the most substantively interesting describe two important features of the social setting: the proportion of agents who are hard-liners, `prop-hard`; and the openness of citizens to interactions with people from different social groups, `out-group-openness`. Our first task, therefore, is to map out the relationship between these two features of the social world and the evolved polarization of public opinion.

If you play with the model, you'll quickly see that after a while the initial random scatter of agents' preferences evolves into a stable distribution of public opinion. We therefore need to estimate how many cycles of the model constitute "a while." Our first experiment is designed to estimate the length of the burn-in era, during which the distribution of preferences in the population is still evolving. As in the first Element in this series, we do this using a small set of very long run repetitions in experiment 1 of the model **Evolution of preferences 1.0**. Figure 2.5 plots output from this.

The top panel shows model output on our key quantity of interest, `net-polar`, over eight very long repetitions – of 20,000 iterations each. This shows output evolving into what looks like a stochastic steady state for each repetition. The bottom panel gives more detail for the first 2,000 iterations of each repetition. This shows model output more or less stabilizing after 1,000 cycles, though still trending for repetition 3. For our purposes, therefore, we're going to treat the first 1,000 cycles as a "good enough" burn-in era for this model. We could be more cautious and set this at 2,000 cycles, but this would halve the number of simulations we can run for the same computational budget. We would be safer still to let model output take 10,000 cycles to burn in, at the cost of only being able to run one-tenth as many simulations. As with so many things in life, sadly there is a law of diminishing marginal returns as we extend the burn-in period; things continue to improve, but at an ever-slower rate. Our results will become more reliable as we increase burn-in, but we will have fewer results for a fixed computational budget. Greedy as we are for results, we will tolerate the relatively short burn-in era of 1,000 model cycles. If we later want more robust industrial-strength results – for example, to publish in a professional journal – we can always rerun our simulations with a longer burn-in. Although the results will almost certainly not change in any substantial way, the confidence with which we present them to others will increase.

Our design for a suite of simulations analyzing the relative impact on evolved polarization of public opinion of the proportion of hardliners, and the openness of citizens to interactions with different social groups, is given in the following Behavior Space specification:

```
["attraction" 0.1]
["hard-bias" 10]
["prop-hard" 0.03 0.05 0.07]
```

```
["reaction" 5]
["n-pinks" 250]
["hard-scatter" 5]
["n-blues" 250]
["out-group-openness" [0 0.01 0.1]]
```

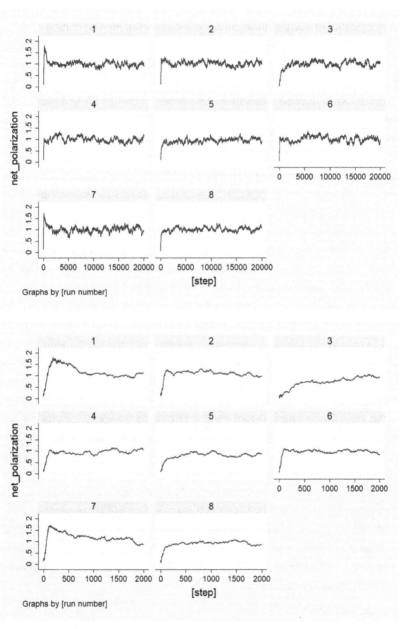

Figure 2.5 Polarization of public opinion; model burn-in

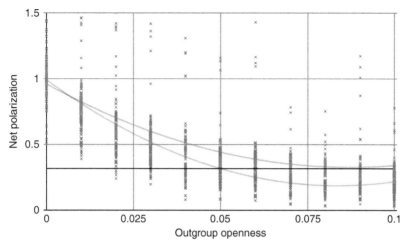

Figure 2.6 Out-group openness and polarization. (Blue, `prop-hard` = .03; red, `prop-hard` = 0.07) Trend lines are second-order polynomial fits

We specify 250 agents from each group and fix `attraction`, `reaction`, `hard-bias`, and `hard-scatter`. We specify a grid sweep of `prop-hard` (setting values at 0.3, 0.5, and 0.7) and `out-group-openness` (increasing values from 0 to 0.1 in increments of 0.01). We specify 50 run repetitions for each of the 3 × 11 = 33 model parameterizations, terminate each of the resulting 1,650 repetitions after a burn-in era of 1,000 iterations, and record values of `net-polar` at the end of each burnt-in repetition. This is experiment 2 of the model **Evolution of preferences 1.0**. Figure 2.6 shows the (nonlinear) results, which for the sake of clarity omit output for model runs with `prop-hard` = 0.5.

We see four things of interest and importance in these results. First, the far left of Figure 2.6 shows the type of outcome we reported in Figure 2.4. When `out-group-openness` is set to zero, so agents never interact with people from a different group, the net polarization of public opinion is distributed symmetrically around 1. In words, when there is no outgroup interaction, the polarization of citizens' opinions systematically converges on the polarization of hardliners. Second, there is more *variation* of polarization when there are fewer hardliners – the blue plot points are much more scattered than the red ones. Theoretically we expect this because evolving group preferences are less anchored when there are fewer hardliners, a general pattern that can be seen here for all levels of `out-group-openness`. Third, as expected, having more hardliners tends to increase net polarization. Polarization when 7 percent of the population are hardliners (plotted in red) is systematically higher than when 3 percent are hardliners (plotted in blue). In a nutshell, and as we expect theoretically, the higher the proportion of hardliners, the bigger effect they have on the evolution of public opinion.

The other striking and informative result we see in Figure 2.6, reading this from left to right, is the *sharp decline in polarization as agents become even slightly more inclined to interact with people from other groups*. For example, with 3 percent hardliners the blue trend line shows that net polarization tends to decline to 0.5 (group members are on average only *half as polarized as their hardliners*) when outgroup openness moves from zero to 0.03 (on average 3 percent of interactions with peers involve members of different social group). By the time out-group-openness has increased to 0.06, net polarization declines to 0.25. The bold horizontal line in Figure 2.6 highlights the relative effects of hardliners and outgroup openness on the evolved polarization of public opinion. When the proportion of hardliners is 0.03 and outgroup openness is 0.05, evolved net polarization is about one third of the polarization of hardliners. If the proportion of hardliners rises to 0.07, however, outgroup openness must double in order to counteract the effect of hardliners and maintain net polarization at the same level. Both theoretically and substantively, these are big and important effects.

The most striking pattern in Figure 2.6 is that even low levels of out-group-openness counteract the polarizing effect of hardliners. We look more closely at this in Figure 2.7. The simulations reported here repeat the previous design but fix the proportion of hardliners at 0.05 and extend the grid sweep of out-group-openness to range from zero to 0.40 in intervals of 0.02. This is experiment 3 of the model **Evolution of preferences 1.0**. By the time out-group-openness reaches 0.20, so one in five peers come from another social group,

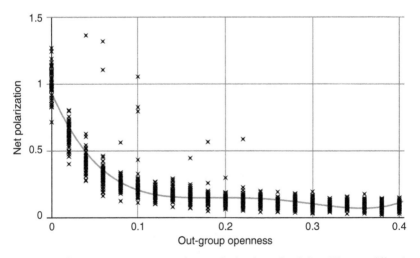

Figure 2.7 Out-group openness and net polarization of opinion. The trend line is a fourth-order polynomial fit

most of the reduction in net polarization has been realized. Polarization is now relatively low, and further increases in `out-group-openness` have only a small effect.

This simple agent-based model of social interaction, using the single page of code in the box at the end of this section, takes us surprisingly far in understanding the evolution of polarized public opinion. We see how repeatedly iterated random social interactions, involving just a hint of group conformity, lead from random scatters of opinions to bell-shaped distributions of these. We see how two groups can evolve to have very different distributions of opinion if there is little or no interaction between groups. We see how distributions of opinion in a group can be anchored by a few group hardliners. Above all, we see how even a small degree of openness to interacting with other social groups can substantially lower polarization. This is the big theoretical and substantive take-home point from the simple baseline model developed and explored in this section. Different social groups with some hardline members may evolve to have polarized distributions of opinion, but this effect is by far the most striking when social interaction between groups is either nonexistent or very limited. *Small increases in intergroup interaction tend to result in big reductions in polarization.* Very crudely this suggests the policy that, if group-based polarization is seen as a problem, then engineering even *slightly* more intergroup interaction, which may not be a hopeless goal, might be more effective than we might superficially expect.

NETLOGO CODE FOR **EVOLUTION OF PREFERENCES 1.0** MODEL
(Not Including Polarization Reporters)

```
;; _____
;;
;;    SETUP AND HOUSEKEEPING
;; _____

breed [citizens citizen]
breed [hardliners hardliner]
turtles-own [group peer]
to setup
  clear-all
  create-citizens n-pinks [set group pink set color pink]
  create-citizens n-blues [set group blue set color sky]
  ask turtles [setxy random-xcor random-ycor]

  ask n-of int (prop-hard * n-pinks) citizens with [group = pink]
    [set breed hardliners
  ask n-of int (prop-hard * n-blues) citizens with [group = blue]
```

```
      [set breed hardliners]
    ask hardliners [biased-scatter set shape "person" set size 2
      set color gray]

    ask patches [set pcolor white]
    reset-ticks
  end

to biased-scatter
  ifelse group = blue
      [setxy random-normal hard-bias hard-scatter random-normal
        hard-bias hard-scatter]
      [setxy random-normal (-1 * hard-bias) hard-scatter
        random-normal (-1 * hard-bias) hard-scatter]
end

;;_____
;;
;; CITIZEN DYNAMICS
;;_____

to go
  ask citizens [
      set peer one-of other turtles
      ifelse [group] of peer = [group] of self
              [interact]
              [if random-float 1 < out-group-openness [interact]]]
    tick
End

to interact
  set heading random-float 360
  forward reaction
  face peer
  forward distance peer * attraction
end
```

3 Evolution of Public Opinion on Social Networks

We just described the evolution of public opinion driven by random social interaction structured by membership of social groups. We assumed that everyone has the same probability of interacting with everyone else from the same group, no matter how large the group. Real social interactions, however, are *not* typically with random strangers from the same group. It is common these days to see social interactions as structured by *networks*; people interact socially with more-or-less familiar network neighbors, who are a small subset of the entire social group. These neighbors in turn interact with their own neighbors, who interact with their own neighbors, and so on. So you interact *indirectly* with strangers who are neighbors of neighbors of neighbors. But your direct interactions are with your own network neighbors. In the language of our baseline model of social interaction, agents' peers are network neighbors, not random strangers.

The most important decision we face when investigating interaction on any social network concerns the network's *structure*, which is a product of systematic patterns that link network neighbors. There are many different types of network structure, and the particular network structure we investigate depends critically on how we expect real humans to interact in the social setting of interest. This is a fundamentally empirical question taking us well beyond the scope of this Element. What I do here is focus on two very different network structures: random and preferential attachment networks. I compare output from models based on these two network structures to show how the choice of network structure has a big impact on outcomes of social interaction.

Random networks structure social interaction in a manner close to the random social interactions modeled in the previous section. In a random network, each agent has the same probability of being a neighbor of any other agent; this connection probability is a key model parameter. If there are 100 agents in a network, for example, and if the connection probability is 0.10, then each agent will on average have 10 network neighbors, although there will be random variation around this number. Note that, despite superficial similarities, social interaction on a random network is *not* the same as random social interaction. With random social interaction, any agent at any time has some chance of interacting with any other agent. With a random network, the choice of network neighbors is random but, once these neighbors are determined, agents can only interact with these, not with any other agent.

Preferential attachment networks have a very different structure, determined by what happens when a new agent joins the network. The probability a new agent connects to any other is proportional to the number of network neighbors each other agent already has. Under this "rich get richer" network structure, agents who already have more network connections become even better connected as the network grows and new entrants connect to them at a higher rate than to less well-connected others. Many see this type of network as common in the real world, for example, on social media.

The number of network connections of any given agent is its *degree*. In random networks, agents' degrees are normally distributed around a mean given by the connection probability. This differs sharply from the degree distribution in a preferential attachment network, which is highly skewed, following a power law. A few agents have many more connections than most others. If people tend to influence network neighbors, then a few agents will have much more influence than most others. We'll soon see that this has a big effect on the evolution of public opinion.

Modeling Social Networks in NetLogo

A nice feature of NetLogo is its "Network" extension. Among many other things this allows you, with one line of code, to set up agents on one of several important types of network, including the random and preferential attachment networks we investigate here. (You can set up "small world," lattice, ring, and star networks just as easily.) Figure 3.1 shows a 100-agent random network, with connection probability 0.02, set up by the NetLogo instruction `nw:generate-random turtles links 100 0.02`. The connection probability of 0.02 was chosen to generate on average the same number of network links as the 100-agent preferential attachment network in Figure 3.2. We now have our agents on a random network. After we create agents, we tell them to move to random locations with the instruction `setxy random-xcor random-ycor`. Little black dots are agents and gray lines are links between them.

Figure 3.2 shows a 100-agent preferential attachment network set up by the NetLogo instruction `nw:generate-preferential-attachment`

Figure 3.1 100-agent random network with connection probability = 0.02

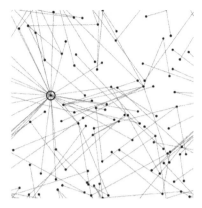

Figure 3.2 100-agent preferential attachment network

`turtles links 100`. (We soon look more closely at this code. The **Network setup demo** is a simple model showing how to create the networks like those shown in Figures 3.1 and 3.2.)

Comparing the two networks, we see crucial differences. The most important is the few *very* highly connected agents in the preferential attachment network, notably the agent to the center-left of Figure 3.2, identified with a circle. We expect these highly connected agents to have an oversized influence on the evolution of public opinion – to be super-influencers.

Another important difference is the existence of completely unconnected agents in the random network, which we see by looking closely at Figure 3.1 for lonely black dots with no links. It's also possible in random networks, especially small ones, to have several completely unconnected subnetworks, subgroups of agents who are connected to others in the subgroup but not to other subgroups. This is not possible in a preferential attachment network, which is grown by starting with one agent and adding new agents using the preferential attachment mechanism.

Now guess which type of network will generate the most polarization of public opinion. Don't leaf forward to results reported later; write your answer now on a slip of paper!

A NetLogo Model of Evolution of Public Opinion on a Network

It's easy to adapt the model from the previous section to describe evolution of public opinion on a network. The structure of the model is a little different, however, since the peers with which each agent interacts are chosen when networks are set up before each model run rather than on the fly during the run itself.

NetLogo's network generation instructions set up breeds of agents who linked on a network. We're going to set up two breeds, "A"s and "B"s, which we're going to color pink and blue respectively. The numbers of pinks and blues, n-pinks and n-blues, are global variables set by sliders on the interface. Before the setup procedure, therefore, we first fire up NetLogo's "Network" extension and declare the breeds of agent we'll create:

```
extensions [nw]
breed [As A]
breed [Bs B]
breed [hardliners hardliner]
```

The setup procedure then creates n-pinks agents from the A breed and puts these on a random network with a connection-probability set by a slider on the interface:

```
to setup
clear-all
nw:generate-random As links n-pinks connection-prob [set color pink]
```

The nw:generate-random command uses the NetLogo network extension to create a random network of new agents. After this, we specify the breed (in this case As) of agent we want to create, and the breed of link we want (in this case the generic links). We then specify the number of agents to be created. This is n-pinks, a global set by a slider on the interface. We then set the connection probability of agents in this random network, given by the global, connection-prob, set by a slider on the interface. We then have a command block for the newly created agents, in this case simply [set color pink]. All of this gives us n-pinks agents on the A-breed random network, with a connection probability specified on the interface.

We use directly analogous code to create a second group, the B-breed colored blue, on their own random network:

```
nw:generate-random Bs links n-blues connection-prob [set color blue]
```

We now have two completely disconnected social networks, populated respectively by A-breed and B-breed agents, colored pink and blue. Next, we model the possibility that agents' social networks contain members of the *other* social group:

```
ask As [if random-float 1 < out-group-openness [create-link-with one-of Bs]]
ask Bs [if random-float 1 < out-group-openness [create-link-with one-of As]]
```

The global variable out-group-openness is set on the interface and has exactly the same meaning as it did in the previous section. It is the probability that an agent interacts with (now, has a network link to) members of another social group. We therefore expand each agent's network with the instruction `create-link-with` a random `one-of` the other group, doing this with probability `out-group-openness`. We then scatter all agents with:

```
ask turtles [set size 1 setxy random-xcor random-ycor]
```

The remainder of the `setup` procedure involves creating hardliners for each group with systematically biased preferences. We do this with precisely the same code as for the model in the previous section. It is important to note here that hardliners are agents who are already on the social networks, so that they may well be peers for other agents.

The hard work has all been done while setting up the networks. The dynamics of the model are now beautifully simple. The `go` procedure that drives the model should be self-evident:

```
to go
  ask turtles with [breed != hardliners] [interact]
end
```

The `interact` procedure is identical to that in the previous section, save that each interaction is with a random network neighbor (`one-of link-neighbors`), conditional on there being such a neighbor (`if peer != nobody`). The instruction `if peer != nobody` is an error trap. Otherwise, when you select an agent with no network neighbors in a random network structure, the code will crash because it tells an agent to face another agent who does not exist. I learned this the hard way. Thus:

```
to interact
  let peer one-of link-neighbors
   if peer != nobody
     [set heading random-float 360
     forward reaction
     face peer
     forward distance peer * attraction]
end
```

Using exactly the same reporters as in the previous section, we now have a complete model of the evolution of public opinion on a random network! This is the model: **Preference network 1.0 random**. Even better, we can now set up the entire model on a preferential attachment network simply by replacing the two lines of network generation code with:

```
nw:generate-preferential-attachment As links n-pinks [set color pink]
nw:generate-preferential-attachment Bs links n-blues [set color blue]
```

This is the model: **Preference network 1.1 preferential attachment**. Analogous code generates any of the other network structures supported by NetLogo, giving you substantial power to analyze effects of network structure on social interaction, which is a hard theoretical problem.

Model Burn-in

The network models we just designed differ in important ways from the model of public opinion we investigated in the previous section so, before designing simulations, we recheck how long it takes the new models to burn in to a stochastic steady state. We follow the procedure set out in earlier Sections, running experiment 1 of the model Preference network 1.0. Detailed results are in the Appendix 3.1. The conclusion we draw from plots in the appendix is to see "good enough" model burn-in after 1,000 iterations in each case. (Bear in mind, 1,000 iterations of the model with 500 agents involves 500,000 simulated social interactions.) We also see that, even after 20,000 iterations when model output has been close to a stochastic steady state for some time, there is still substantial variation around the long run mean of our key output of interest, the net polarization of opinion. This means we need multiple run repetitions for a given parameter setting before we can reliably characterize output for this.

Analyzing Evolution of Public Opinion on a Network

We want to find out how network structure affects the evolution of public opinion. We do this by replicating, for each network model, the simulation design that generated the output reported in Figure 2.6 in the previous section.[3] Screen shots in Figure 3.3 give a taste of the headline results. The evolution of public opinion depends *radically* on whether agents interact on random or preferential attachment networks.

---

[3] With 50 repetitions of each run and a repetition length of 1,000 iterations, this is:

```
["attraction" 0.1]
["hard-bias" 10]
["prop-hard" 0.05]
["reaction" 5]
["n-pinks" 250]
["hard-scatter" 5]
["n-blues" 250]
["out-group-openness" [0 0.02 0.4]]
```

The *connection-probability* for the random network was set to 0.025.
This is experiment 2 of the models Preference network 1.0 and Preference network 1.1.

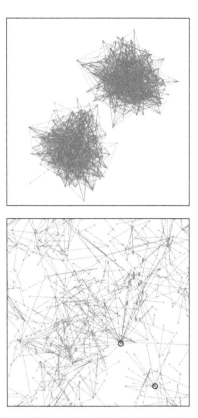

Figure 3.3 Screen shots of burnt-in evolved polarization of public opinion on random (top panel) and preferential attachment (bottom panel) networks, after 5,000 iterations

Evolved public opinion for the random network (top panel) looks quite like that for the random interaction model in the previous section. Results (bottom panel) for the preferential attachment network look very different; evolved polarization of public opinion is *much* less striking for the preferential attachment network for reasons that become clear if we look closely at Figure 3.3. Systematic polarization is generated in the random interaction model because each group's hardliners have distinctive opinions and never change these during social interaction. This effect is moderated by interactions between members of different social groups but, absent this, we see evolution toward complete polarization. The same thing happens with random networks, moderated by the fact that while many agents will not themselves have hardliners as network neighbors, they will typically have indirect links via neighbors, and via neighbors of neighbors, to hardliners on their network. The top panel of Figure 3.3 also shows evolution toward complete polarization in this setting.

The bottom panel shows a very different story for agents interacting on preferential attachment networks. We see that the very highly connected superinfluencer agents act as a strong counterweight to hardliners, pulling agents with whom they interact away from the opinions of the hardliners. Look at the two blue superinfluencers circled in black in the lower right quadrant of the bottom panel of Figure 3.3, located well away from the blue hardliners, shown as little blue men. Other agents are *much* more likely to interact with the superinfluencers than a less well-connected hardliner. Their opinions therefore evolve toward those of super-influencers and away from hardliners. In addition, superinfluencers are typically surrounded by others who interact with them from many different positions, with the net effect that the opinions of superinfluencers are less likely to evolve in any systematic direction. This is not because superinfluencers are inherently obdurate, like hardliners, but because they interact with many different types of people. In this sense the superinfluencers reflect as much as lead public opinion.

If you take the view that superinfluencers lead rather than reflect the *zeitgeist*, then you could modify the preferential attachment model to make them more like hardliners, who influence others but are influenced by nobody. To do this you must specify and code how much like hardliners they are and what, if anything, influences their tastes.

Figure 3.4 reports results of replicating simulations reported in Section 2, modeling the evolution of public opinion with random social interactions and 5 percent hardliners, but with interactions structured on random and preferential attachment networks. Looking first at results for random networks, plotted in red, we see that, as in Figure 2.6 for fully random interactions, net polarization is on average 1.0 when outgroup-openness = 0 and there is no interaction between groups. As before, polarization declines steeply for small increases in the rate of interaction with other groups before leveling off.

The big news in Figure 3.4, previewed in Figure 3.3, is that evolved polarization of public opinion is *much* lower with preferential attachment than with random networks. If there is no interaction between social groups, there is about half as much polarization on preferential attachment networks as on random networks. Polarization is substantially lower on preferential attachment networks for all levels of social interaction.

We already speculated that this is because highly connected superinfluencers in preferential attachment networks act as substantial counterweights to

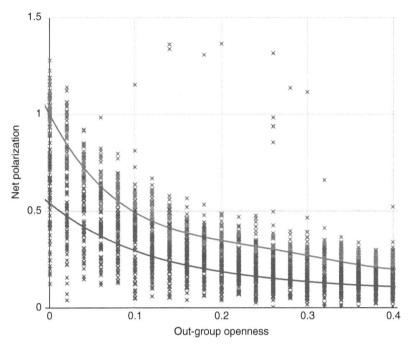

Figure 3.4 Out-group openness and net polarization of opinion on random (red) and preferential attachment (blue) networks. Trend lines are fourth-order polynomial fits

the polarizing effects of hardliners. We investigate this possibility more fully in a further suite of simulations: experiment 3 of the model Preference network 1.1. Results are reported in Figure 3.5. These map out the relationship between proportions of hardliners in a preferential attachment network and evolved net polarization, for two levels of out-group-openness: 0.0 and 0.1.

We saw from Figure 3.4 that, with no interaction between groups and 5 percent hardliners, evolved net polarization in a random network averages 1.0. Citizens' opinions evolve to be as polarized as those of their groups' hardliners. The blue plot in Figure 3.5 shows that, even if 20 percent of agents on a preferential attachment network are hardliners, we do not get close to that level of evolved polarization, which averages out at less than 0.9. Figure 3.4 shows that, when out-group-openness is 0.1, evolved net polarization in a random network averages out at about 0.5. The red plot in Figure 3.5 shows that, with out-group-openness at 0.1, about 13 percent of agents must be hardliners, as opposed to 5 percent, to generate the same level of polarization. Overall, therefore, *relatively small numbers of highly connected*

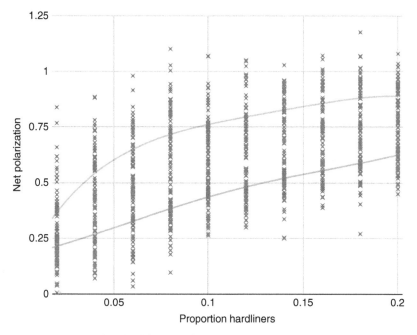

Figure 3.5 Proportion hardliners and net polarization of opinion on preferential attachment networks with out-group openness 0 (blue) and 0.1 (red). Trend lines are fourth-order polynomial fits[4]

superinfluencers in a preferential attachment network can counteract the effects on the polarization of public opinion of relatively large numbers of hardliners.

This section shows that agent-based modeling is ideally suited to answering some hard questions that would confound most alternative approaches to theoretical modeling. There is an exploding volume of literature on the effects of social networks on public opinion, though most of this is empirical and descriptive rather than rigorously analytical. While many might speculate about the different effects

---

[4] Behavior Space code for the simulations is:

```
["attraction" 0.1]
["hard-bias" 10]
["prop-hard" [0.02 0.02 0.2]]
["reaction" 5]
["n-pinks" 250]
["hard-scatter" 5]
["n-blues" 250]
["out-group-openness" 0 0.1]
```

of different types of network on the endogenous evolution of public opinion, we have seen here that agent-based modeling offers a way to provide rigorously derived and replicable answers. The formal analysis of these questions is very hard, but attacking them using an agent-based model is surprisingly simple, especially using the set of network structures supported by NetLogo. Initial results on this, reported in Figures 3.3, 3.4, and 3.5, are striking. We see systematically that network structure makes a big difference. Superinfluencers in preferential attachment networks, unless they are themselves also hardliners, substantially moderate effects of hardliners on evolved polarization of public opinion.

We are just scratching the surface here, and many new problems cry out for investigation. What if, for example, superinfluencers on preferential attachment networks are all hardliners with distinctive distributions of preferences? We can speculate this will amplify the evolution of polarized public opinion, but this is now easy to investigate rigorously with simple modifications to the model (suggested earlier as an exercise for the reader). We can easily give different social groups different types of network structure. We can refine in-network interactions by giving agents other properties that make interactions more likely. We could do this easily by modifying the `interact` procedure to, for example:

```
let peer one-of link-neighbors with [property >= threshold]
```

Here, `property`, which might well also evolve endogenously as the model iterates, would be an agent-specific variable measuring something that conditions social interaction; `threshold` would be a global variable specifying some minimum level of `property`, below which interaction does not take place. This gives you huge flexibility to modify the structure of network interactions in ways that seem plausible to you.

The bottom line here is that the NetLogo network extension gives you tremendous firepower with which to attack previously intractable questions about the evolving effects of social interaction on a wide range of important matters.

4 Public Opinion with Crosscutting Group Memberships

Up to now we have modeled the evolution of public attitudes using the strong assumption that membership of groups structuring social interaction is *exclusive* – that everyone belongs to one group or another but not to two groups at the same time. We modeled social interaction between people in different groups, but not the possibility that one person belongs to several groups.

There may, for example, be two or more different language groups in a society – as with French and German native speakers in Switzerland. People may naturally be more likely to interact socially with others who speak the same language than with those who speak a different language. On top of this, people

Table 4.1 Societies with crosscutting and reinforcing group memberships

XC = 0.50	Language A	Language B	Total
Village 1	1,000	1,000	2,000
Village 2	1,000	1,000	2,000
Total	2,000	2,000	4,000
XC = 0.00	**Language A**	**Language B**	**Total**
Village 1	2,000	0	2,000
Village 2	0	2,000	2,000
Total	2,000	2,000	4,000

who live in one of two small villages may well be more likely to interact, other things being equal (and we'll see shortly what might not be equal), with others from the same village than with those living in a different village. Everyone's native tongue is either language A or language B; everyone lives in either village 1 or village 2. Everyone now belongs to two groups that structure social interaction. A key feature of this social structure is whether group memberships overlap or cut across each other.

Consider two very different societies described in the top and bottom panels of Table 4.1. Both have the same number of people. In each, people are split evenly between two language groups and two villages. The two societies have very different social structures, however.

In the top society, group memberships perfectly *cut across* each other – there is the same number from each language group in each village. Two people from the same village who meet at random are equally likely to speak the same, or a different, language. Two people from the same language group are equally likely to meet someone from the same, or a different, village. Knowing your village, it's impossible to predict your language; knowing your language, it's impossible to predict your village.

In the society shown in the bottom panel of Figure 4.1, in stark contrast, group memberships perfectly *reinforce* each other. People meeting others from the same village only ever meet people speaking the same language. People meeting others speaking the same language only ever meet neighbors from the same village. Knowing your native tongue, I can perfectly predict your village, and vice versa.

Differences between these two social structures can have a striking impact on the evolution of individual attitudes. The sociologist Georg Simmel described

Table 4.2 A society with partially crosscutting group memberships

XC = 0.25	Language A	Language B	Total
Village 1	1,500	500	2,000
Village 2	500	1,500	2,000
Total	2,000	2,000	4,000

this phenomenon about 100 years ago, and others have discussed it over the years since then.[5] If group memberships perfectly reinforce each other, as in the bottom society in Table 4.1, it is as if there was only one pair of groups. Village neighbors always have the same native tongue; people from the other village always have a different native tongue. With a social structure like this, we expect polarization of attitudes to evolve in ways similar to the evolution we modeled in Sections 2 and 3. Everyone belongs to two different groups but, since the groups have perfectly overlapping memberships, they might as well belong only to one group. Repeated social interactions systematically tend to pull individual attitudes in the same direction.

When group memberships cut across each other, however, social interaction is very different. Now, individual attitudes are often pulled in different directions as people interact with peers from different social groups. You interact with someone from the same village, who pulls you in one direction. Then you interact with someone with the same native tongue but a different village, who might pull you in a different direction.

Crosscutting group memberships are not the all-or-nothing phenomena we see in Table 4.1 but rather a matter of degree. Table 4.2 shows a society where there is neither total crosscutting nor total reinforcement of group memberships, but a limited degree of crosscutting. Two people from the same village who meet at random have a 25 percent chance of meeting someone with a different native tongue and a 75 percent chance of meeting someone with the same one. Rae and Taylor[6] used these probabilities to define an index of crosscutting for any society. Their index (XC) is precisely the probability that two people chosen at random will

---

[5] Simmel, Georg 1955 [1923] Conflict and the Web of Group Affiliations. Glencoe: Free Press. Blau, P. M. and Schwartz, J. E., 1984. *Crosscutting social circles: Testing a macrostructural theory of intergroup relations.* New York: Academic Press. Chandra, K., 2005. Ethnic parties and democratic stability. *Perspectives on Politics, 3*(2), pp. 235–52. Rokkan, S., 1967. Geography, religion, and social class: Crosscutting cleavages in Norwegian politics. *Party systems and voter alignments, 367,* pp. 379–86.

[6] Rae, D. W. and Taylor, M., 1970. *The analysis of political cleavages.* New Haven, CT: Yale University Press.

be in the same group on one dimension of group cleavage (language group or village in our example) but in different groups on the other dimension. The minimum value of XC is zero when group memberships perfectly reinforce each other, as in the bottom panel of Table 4.1. With two equal-sized pairs of groups such as we find in Table 4.1, the maximum value of crosscutting, XC, is 0.5, since the probability two people from the same village speak different languages is 0.5. Between these extremes, the level of crosscutting group membership in Table 4.2 is 0.25.

Modeling the Impact of Crosscutting Group Memberships on the Evolution of Public Opinion

Despite much theoretical discussion of the effect of crosscutting group memberships on the evolution of social polarization, I'm not aware of an explicit formal model, computational or otherwise, of this important social process. We are now, however, in a position to build such a model, extending models of the evolution of public opinion developed in the previous two sections. Instead of specifying two social groups, we now specify two *pairs* of groups. The first pair splits the population into two groups on one dimension of social interaction, for example, language. The second splits the same population into two groups on a different dimension of social interaction, for example, village. The extent to which these group memberships reinforce or cut across each other is determined by an important new model parameter, xc, the degree of crosscutting, which we specify as Rae and Taylor's XC index.

The NetLogo model of the evolution of individual attitudes with crosscutting group memberships, once two citizens meaningfully interact, is *exactly* the same as in the previous two sections. The impact of interactions with hardliners is also exactly the same, though it is important to note that hardliners' attitudes are defined in relation to the first (or primary) cleavage dimension. While it is possible to conceive of multidimensional polarization, we typically think of polarization on some primary dimension of social cleavage, and this is my approach here. This could obviously be refined to take account of some well-specified concept of multidimensional polarization, although I am not aware of such a concept.

What changes is the relative *likelihood* of particular types of social interactions when there are crosscutting group memberships. This likelihood now depends on whether a given pair of citizens share the same position on two, one, or zero dimensions of social interaction. If they share the same position on both dimensions, then we assume they always interact socially when they meet – just as if they were in the same group in our previous two-group society. If they share the same position on just one dimension, then we assume they interact with probability `outgroup-openness`, which is exactly the same model parameter as in the previous two sections. If they do not share the same position on any dimension, then we assume they interact with the much smaller probability `outgroup-openness ^ 2`, outgroup openness squared. An alternative assumption would be to set the probability of interacting at zero when there is no shared group membership. This would obviously somewhat increase the level of evolved polarization. The effect would be small, however, since `outgroup-openness ^ 2` is typically a very small number. The new model elaborates the evolution of public opinion, given social interactions conditioned by potentially crosscutting group memberships.

A NetLogo Model of the Effect on Public Opinion of Crosscutting Group Memberships

The full NetLogo model of evolving public opinion with crosscutting group memberships is in Appendix 4.1. Most of the new stuff is in the `setup` routine. This assigns citizens to one of two groups, 0 or 1, on each of two dimensions, a or b, of social cleavage. This gives citizens four possible positions in a 2×2 table of social structure analogous to those in Tables 4.1 and 4.2. The proportions of citizens in group 0 on cleavages a and b, respectively, are given by the globals `cleavage-a-mean` and `cleavage-b-mean`, set by sliders on the interface. The first thing to do is to set the *number of citizens* in each cell of the social structure table. The NetLogo operator `round` rounds the result of `cleavage-a-mean * n-pop` to the nearest whole number.

```
set a0 round (cleavage-a-mean * n-pop)
set a1 n-pop – a0
set b0 round (cleavage-b-mean * n-pop)
set b1 n-pop – b0
```

Agents are now given *positions* on `cleavage-a`. Using a common coding device, we do this by first giving all agents position 0, then moving a random selection of a1 citizens to position 1.

```
ask citizens [set cleavage-a 0]
ask n-of a1 citizens [set cleavage-a 1]
```

A key feature of the model is that citizens are given positions on `cleavage-b`, *conditional on their positions on* `cleavage-a`, according to the level of crosscutting group memberships, xc, a critical new global variable set by a slider on the interface. This is where crosscutting group memberships enter the model:

```
ask citizens with [cleavage-a = 0] [set cleavage-b 0]
ask n-of (a0 * xc) citizens with [cleavage-a = 0] [set cleavage-b 1]
ask citizens with [cleavage-a = 1] [set cleavage-b 1]
ask n-of (a1 * xc) citizens with [cleavage-a = 1] [set cleavage-b 0]
```

Each agent's position in this table is then stored in its `subgroup` variable, which can take the values $00, 01, 10, 11$. At the same time, we give members of each subgroup a distinctive `color` to make them easier to keep track of on the interface.

```
ask citizens [
  if (cleavage-a = 1 and cleavage-b = 1) [set subgroup 11 set color blue]
  if (cleavage-a = 1 and cleavage-b = 0) [set subgroup 10 set color cyan]
  if (cleavage-a = 0 and cleavage-b = 1) [set subgroup 01 set color pink]
  if (cleavage-a = 0 and cleavage-b = 0) [set subgroup 00 set color red]]
```

The `interact` procedure itself is *exactly* the same as in previous models. *What makes a given pair of agents interact*, however, is more complicated in the model with crosscutting group memberships. We find this in a more complicated `go` procedure, which by now should be self-explanatory:

```
to go
  ask citizens [

  set peer one-of other turtles

                ;; if a and b categories the same, interact
  if ([cleavage-a] of peer = [cleavage-a] of self and
     [cleavage-b] of peer = [cleavage-b] of self) [interact]

                ;; if peer is same category on a but not on b
                ;; interact with probability outgroup-openness
  if ([cleavage-a] of peer = [cleavage-a] of self and
     [cleavage-b] of peer != [cleavage-b] of self)
     [if (random-float 1 < outgroup-openness) [interact]]

                ;; and vice versa
  if ([cleavage-a] of peer != [cleavage-a] of self and
     [cleavage-b] of peer = [cleavage-b] of self)
     [if (random-float 1 < outgroup-openness) [interact]]

                ;; if peer is same category on neither
                ;; interact with probability outgroup-openness ^ 2
  if ([cleavage-a] of peer != [cleavage-a] of self and
     [cleavage-b] of peer != [cleavage-b] of self)
```

```
    [if (random-float 1 < outgroup-openness ^ 2) [interact]]
  tick
end
```

I could very likely streamline this rather plodding procedure, and you might take this on as an exercise, but the current code does benefit from legibility. Our key *output of interest* remains evolved polarization in public opinion, which we expect from the extensive literature on this topic and our previous discussion to be less severe when the crosscutting of group memberships is higher. Thinking more carefully about this, however, there are at least two types of polarization to consider when we try to understand the impact on public opinion of crosscutting group memberships.

Returning to the bottom panel of Table 4.1, with no crosscutting of group memberships, there are two dominant groups. No member of either group will ever encounter someone from another group, and therefore none of them will experience cross-pressure. In the less extreme situation in Table 4.2, with some but not complete crosscutting of group memberships, we see two larger dominant subgroups, in the top left and bottom right cells of the table, and two smaller subgroups, in the top right and bottom left. Agents in the two dominant subgroups are less likely to encounter people with different group affiliations and are therefore less likely to be cross-pressured. In contrast, people in the nondominant subgroups are *more* likely to encounter people with different group affiliations and therefore are more likely to be cross-pressured.

Given this, we define two additional measures of polarization that distinguish between members of the two dominant subgroups, and members of the less dominant and more cross-pressured subgroups. Theoretically, we expect dominant subgroup polarization to be higher than nondominant subgroup polarization, since members of nondominant subgroups are systematically more cross-pressured. This difference should disappear, with equal-sized groups on each cleavage, when there is perfect crosscutting of group memberships, since all citizens will be cross-pressured to the same degree.

Two new NetLogo reporters capture this distinction:

```
to-report dom-polarization        ;; polarization of dominant subgroups
                                   ;; normed by polarization of hardliners

  let x00 mean [xcor] of turtles with [subgroup = 00]
  let y00 mean [ycor] of turtles with [subgroup = 00]
```

```
    let x11 mean [xcor] of turtles with [subgroup = 11]
    let y11 mean [ycor] of turtles with [subgroup = 11]
    let norm sqrt ((2 * hard-bias) ^ 2 + (2 * hard-bias) ^ 2)
    report sqrt ((x00 - x11) ^ 2 + (y00 - y11) ^ 2) / norm
end

to-report nondom-polarization
                            ;; polarization of non-dom. Subgroups
                            ;; normed by polarization of hardliners
    let x01 mean [xcor] of turtles with [subgroup = 01]
    let y01 mean [ycor] of turtles with [subgroup = 01]
    let x10 mean [xcor] of turtles with [subgroup = 10]
    let y10 mean [ycor] of turtles with [subgroup = 10]
    let norm sqrt ((2 * hard-bias) ^ 2 + (2 * hard-bias) ^ 2)
    report sqrt ((x01 - x10) ^ 2 + (y01 - y10) ^ 2) / norm
end
```

To maintain comparability with results from previous sections as well as provide easily interpretable summary results, we also define a reporter to measure overall polarization.

```
to-report polarization
                    ;; polarization normed by polarization of hardliners
    let x0 mean [xcor] of turtles with [cleavage-a = 0]
    let y0 mean [ycor] of turtles with [cleavage-a = 0]
    let x1 mean [xcor] of turtles with [cleavage-a = 1]
    let y1 mean [ycor] of turtles with [cleavage-a = 1]
    let norm sqrt ((2 * hard-bias) ^ 2 + (2 * hard-bias) ^ 2)
    report sqrt ((x0 - x1) ^ 2 + (y0 - y1) ^ 2) / norm
end
```

This is a linear function of the previous two measures and therefore contains no new information:

```
polarization = xc * nondom-polarization + (1 - xc) * dom-polarization.
```

The resulting NetLogo model is **Preference XC 1.0.**

Results

Appendix 4.2 gives burn-in diagnostics for the crosscutting model with 5 percent hardliners and 5 percent `outgroup-openness`, for three levels of crosscutting: a very low 0.05, a moderate 0.25, and the maximum 0.50. This is experiment 1 of the model **Preference XC 1.0**. Note that, when `outgroup-openness = 0`, crosscutting group memberships by construction have no effect whatsoever on the evolution of individual attitudes. The effect of crosscutting group memberships depends on at least some minimal level of outgroup openness. Plots show eight very long (20,000-cycle) diagnostic replications for each parameterization as well as the first 2,000 cycles of this. Model outputs look close to burnt-in after 1,000 cycles and with "good enough" burn-in after 2,000 cycles, the duration selected for each production run reported below.

We see early evidence from the burn-in plots to support our expectation that both measures of polarization will converge at the maximum possible level of crosscutting (xc = 0.50). However, we also see, for the full set of 20,000 diagnostic repetitions with xc = 0.50, that model output remains somewhat path-dependent and not fully ergodic. In repetitions 2 and 3, for example, dominant-group polarization remains stuck steadfastly above that of nondominant groups, whereas in repetition 5 the reverse is the case. The two measures of polarization are effectively indistinguishable in repetitions 4, 6, and 7. We therefore need to aggregate results from multiple run repetitions to get reliable estimates of output quantities. We cannot rule out the possibility that outputs of interest would have converged completely across multiple ultralong run repetitions of well over 20,000 cycles. With the information at our disposal, however, aggregating results across multiple 2,000-cycle repetitions seems the best run design.

The first substantive computational experiment systematically investigates the general theoretical argument that higher levels of crosscutting, associated with more cross-pressuring of agents, lead to lower levels of polarization. This involves 100 repetitions of each of 11 run parameterizations, varying xc from 0.00 to 0.50 in increments of 0.05.[7] Figure 4.1 shows the headline result in black. As many scholars have argued theoretically, evolved polarization of attitudes does indeed decrease steadily as crosscutting of group memberships increases. It is close to its maximum possible level when there is no crosscutting; it reaches a much lower level, about a third of the maximum, when crosscutting is as high as theoretically possible.

Figure 4.1 digs deeper, however. Increased crosscutting has *very* different effects for members of the more (red) and less (blue) dominant subgroups. We see the expected effect for the more dominant subgroups. Higher levels of crosscutting increase the probability of meeting someone from a different group, increasing cross-pressures and leading to *less* polarization of attitudes.

---

[7] The full Behavior Space run parameterization for this, experiment 2 of the model **Preference XC 1.0**, was:

["cleavage-a-mean" 0.5] ["cleavage-b-mean" 0.5] ["attraction" 0.1] ["hard-bias" 20]
  ["outgroup-openness" 0.05]
["prop-hard" 0.05] ["n-pop" 500] ["reaction" 2] ["xc" [0 0.05 0.5]]

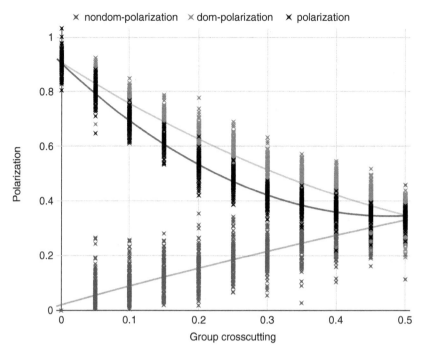

Figure 4.1 Evolved polarization of public opinion by group crosscutting, 5 percent hardliners. Trend lines are second-order polynomial fits

The effect for less-dominant subgroups is less obvious intuitively, since increased crosscutting is associated with *more* polarization of attitudes. Scholars writing on crosscutting group memberships have not, to my knowledge, discussed this.

Without using an agent-based model such as this, it is difficult to investigate in a systematic way the effects of increased crosscutting on subsections of the population. Thinking things through, this pattern likely arises because, with low levels of crosscutting, *less-dominant subgroups are relatively small*. This means their members are almost always cross-pressured, since their typical interactions are with members of other subgroups, with whom they must differ on at least one group membership. As crosscutting increases in a population of the same size, the size of less-dominant subgroups increases, paradoxically *reducing* the extent to which their members are cross-pressured, since they are now *more* likely to encounter peers who share both group memberships. The resulting increase in in-group interaction has the effect of increasing polarization between the less-dominant subgroups. Nevertheless, polarization between the

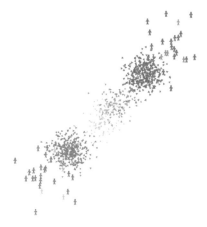

Figure 4.2 Stochastic steady-state polarization of public opinion after 5,000 cycles with XC = 0.25. (Proportion hardliners = 0.05, equal-sized groups on each cleavage, dominant subgroups have darker shading)

cross-pressured nondominant groups is typically lower than that between dominant groups.

Figure 4.2 shows another way of looking at this, with a screenshot of an evolved stochastic steady state of public opinion after 5,000 iterations of the model in a society with an intermediate level of crosscutting (xc = 0.25). This shows the different contributions of dominant and nondominant subgroups to reduced polarization in such a setting. The dominant subgroups (darker shading) are less cross-pressured and so stay closer to their hardliners, though the existence of some cross-pressuring drags both dominant groups somewhat toward the center. There is less movement in attitudes arising from crosscutting group memberships, but there are more agents who move. The (lightly shaded) less-dominant subgroups are more likely to be cross-pressured and are therefore more likely to move toward the center. There is more movement in attitudes toward the center in these subgroups, but fewer agents move. Hardliners of any stripe, by assumption, never move.

Since cross-pressures generated by crosscutting group memberships tend to counter the effect of hardliners in polarizing public opinion, the big question concerns the interacting effects of hardliners and crosscutting on evolved polarization of public opinion. We investigate this with an experiment that varies both xc and prop-hard at the same time. We modify the experiment

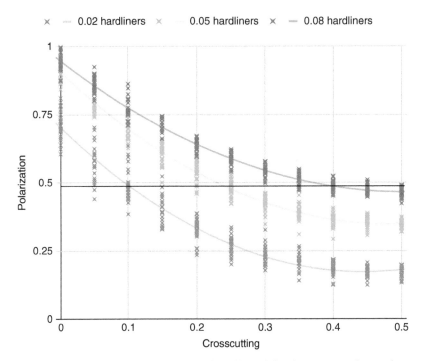

Figure 4.3 Evolved polarization of public opinion by crosscutting and proportion hardliners. Trend lines are second-order polynomial fits

reported in Figure 4.1 to specify low (0.02), medium (0.05), and high (0.08) levels of prop-hard, with 25 run repetitions per parameterization.[8] Figure 4.3 plots the results.

Taking polarization with intermediate setting of xc = 0.25 and prop-hard = 0.05 as a benchmark, reading along the black horizontal line shows us that increasing the level of crosscutting from 0.25 to 0.45 counteracts the effect on polarization of having 8 percent rather than 5 percent hardliners. Conversely, if there are only 2 percent hardliners, a much lower level of crosscutting (0.10) generates the same level of polarization. *Both the proportion of hardliners and the level of crosscutting have substantial effects on evolved polarization of public opinion.* Comparing blue and red plots, for example, the horizontal black line shows that the effect of quadrupling the proportion of hardliners from 0.02 to 0.08 is reversed by quadrupling the

---

[8]   The full Behavior Space design for experiment 3 of the model **Preference CX 1.0** was:

["prop-hard" 0.02 0.05 0.08] ["xc" [0 0.05 0.5]] ["cleavage-a-mean" 0.5] ["cleavage-b-mean" 0.5] ["hard-bias" 20]
["outgroup-openness" 0.05] ["n-pop" 500] ["attraction" 0.1] ["reaction" 2]

degree of crosscutting, from 0.1 to 0.4. Similarly, comparing blue and green plots, increasing the proportion of hardliners by a factor of 2.5 from 0.02 to 0.05, is counteracted by increasing the level of crosscutting by a factor of 2.5 from 0.10 to 0.25.

We know theoretically that even strongly crosscutting group memberships have no effect whatsoever on the evolution of public opinion if people only ever interact with others who share all group memberships, if outgroup-openness = 0. Most theoretical discussions of the effects of crosscutting group memberships informally rely on the idea that individual attitudes may be affected by interactions with others who share *some but not all* group memberships. In results reported so far, we fixed outgroup-openness at 0.05, but this is clearly a key model parameter. We now investigate its effects with an experiment that varies both xc and outgroup-openness at the same time, holding prop-hard constant at 0.05. We modify the experiment reported in Figure 4.2 to specify low (0.02), medium (0.05), and high (0.08) levels of outgroup-openness, with 25 run repetitions per parameterization.[9] Figure 4.4 plots the results.

We see the now-familiar pattern in which higher levels of crosscutting are associated with lower evolved polarization of public opinion. But we now also see that openness to interaction with outgroups plays a big part in this. The red plot shows that, with outgroup-openness as low as 0.02 (agents have only a one in fifty chance of interacting with others who do not share all group memberships), increased crosscutting still has a substantial effect on the evolved polarization of public opinion. The black horizontal line shows that evolved polarization with maximum crosscutting is about half that arising with no crosscutting at all. However, when outgroup-openness increases to 0.05, giving agents a one in twenty chance of interacting with others who do not share all group memberships, the green plot shows that *much* lower levels of crosscutting (xc = 0.20) are needed to generate the same evolved polarization of public opinion.

We draw two substantively important lessons from these results. First, increased openness to meaningful social interactions with members of outgroups and increased crosscutting of group memberships are both strongly associated with lower evolved polarization of social attitudes. Second, and

---

[9] Thus the full Behavior Space design for experiment 4 of the model **Preference XC 1.0** was:

["outgroup-openness" 0.02 0.05 0.08] ["xc" [0 0.05 0.5]] ["cleavage-a-mean" 0.5]
    ["cleavage-b-mean" 0.5]
["attraction" 0.1] ["hard-bias" 20] ["prop-hard" 0.05] ["n-pop" 500] ["reaction" 2]

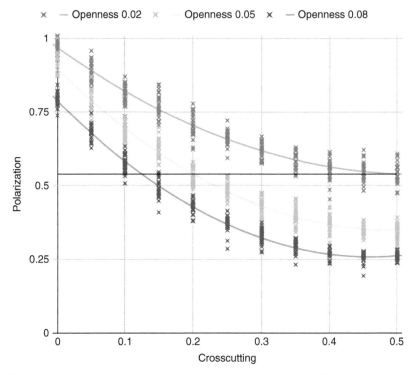

Figure 4.4 Evolved polarization of public opinion by crosscutting and outgroup
openness. Trend lines are second-order polynomial fits

reinforcing longstanding informal arguments in the literature, *even with very
little openness to interacting with others who do not share all group
memberships*, increased crosscutting of group memberships is associated
with big reductions in the evolved polarization of public opinion.

Conclusions

Putting all of this together, we now have a formal computational model that both
supports and digs deeper into informal but influential theoretical arguments
about the impact of crosscutting group memberships on the evolved polarization of public opinion. The results presented in this section are good examples of
substantively important findings that would have been difficult to derive using
traditional methods, but are easily generated using agent-based models. These
results give a firmer formal foundation to the informal general argument that
crosscutting social cleavages, by cross-pressuring people when they interact
socially, tend to reduce the evolved polarization of attitudes. The black trend
line in Figure 4.1 illustrates this.

The real payoffs extend well beyond underpinning existing informal arguments. We now have at our mercy a working formal model of these cross-pressures. For example, the red and blue trend lines in Figure 4.1 show that cross-pressures have radically different effects on different subgroups, which is a new finding. The informal intuition about the reduction of polarization as crosscutting increases applies to what I've called the two dominant subgroups. But the pattern is actually *reversed* for members of the off-diagonal minority subgroups that must logically emerge when we move from a situation with no crosscutting at all to one with low levels of crosscutting. Members of these subgroups are almost totally cross-pressured when the subgroups are very small. They become less cross-pressured as crosscutting increases because the minority subgroups increase in size, making their members more likely to interact with people exactly like themselves and thereby increasing polarization. This is an interesting new finding.

It's always been the case that informal theoretical arguments about the effects of crosscutting cleavages have relied on an assumption, typically unstated, that people are affected by interactions with others who share some but not all their group memberships. One of the massive advantages of computational models is that we must specify everything very precisely before the model will even run. Here, we see that there is what amounts to a hidden parameter in the informal argument, which is the *extent* to which people are influenced by social interactions with others who share some but not all group memberships. For our agent-based model to work, we have to specify this parameter, which is outgroup-openness. This allows us to conduct systematic investigations of the interaction between outgroup-openness and the level of crosscutting, with results reported in Figure 4.4. We are still only scratching the surface, but we now have a model that can be modified, extended, and tortured, almost without limit, to allow us to dig deeper into a social phenomenon that has long been seen as important, but which has yet to be subjected to rigorous formal analysis.

5 Does "Ethnocentrism" Pay?

We looked in the first Element of this pair (Agent-Based Models of Social Life: Fundamentals) at social segregation, in particular the striking effects of even modest preferences for living close to other people from the same social group. We looked earlier in this Element at striking impacts on the polarization of attitudes if people are more likely to interact with others from the same social group than with others. We now turn to a thornier and more sensitive problem. Is it in any sense rational to interact positively with others from the same social group and negatively with others? Does this type of "ethnocentric" behavior pay?

We attack this question by investigating and torturing an influential agent-based model of "ethnocentric" behavior. Hammond and Axelrod, the authors of this model, conclude that ethnocentrism does indeed pay, defining ethnocentric behavior as cooperating with individuals from your own social group, but not with those of other groups. They find that "in-group favoritism can be an undemanding yet powerful mechanism for supporting high levels of individually costly cooperation with only minimal cognitive requirements" (p. 932).[10]

This model is more complicated than others we've worked with so far and takes us into important new territory. It describes an *evolutionary* environment in which agents have different types, or species, defined by the decision rules that determine their behavior when they interact with others. These include altruists, who always cooperate with others regardless of who they are, and egoists, who never cooperate with others in any circumstance. Crucially, there are also "ethnocentrics," who condition their cooperation on the social group of the person they interact with; they cooperate with other people from the same group but refuse to cooperate with people from other groups.

The environment we model is evolutionary. Some agents die and some are born at each cycle of the model. Agents of different species replicate themselves in the next generation with a probability proportional to their success in the previous cycle. Evolution happens because the more successful agents, those using more effective decision rules, are more likely to replicate in the next generation. As with all evolution, there is also a small probability of random mutations or mistakes, which have the effect that new agents' children do not have the same type as their parent, but a random different type. All this will become a lot clearer when we get into the model, but the basic idea is that subpopulations of the more successful types of agent prosper and grow, while the reverse is true for less successful types of agent.

The bottom line in Hammond and Axelrod's results is that "ethnocentric" agents are the ones who typically prosper because they are rewarded for their ethnocentric behavior and reproduce at a faster rate. As we soon see when we torture the model, however, this finding is brittle – easily broken by small but plausible changes in key assumptions. In what follows, therefore, we learn not only how to set up an evolutionary environment in an agent-based model, which is a very useful piece of technology in itself, but also how to assess the sensitivity of key theoretical findings from the model to small and essentially arbitrary

---

[10] Hammond, R. A. and R. Axelrod (2006). "The evolution of ethnocentrism." *Journal of Conflict Resolution* **50**: 926–36.

assumptions. First, however, we turn to the Prisoners' Dilemma Game, which is a very common way to model tensions between conflict and cooperation in many different types of social setting.

Modeling Incentives for Cooperation Using the Prisoners' Dilemma Game

Originally formulated in 1950 by Merrill Flood and Melvin Dresher, two mathematicians working for the RAND Corporation, the Prisoners' Dilemma (PD) game is now a classic way to model interactions between agents who face the mixed motives of conflict and cooperation. I briefly set out the game for those who don't already know it, then describe how it can be used to model ethnocentrism.

The original story is of two prisoners arrested for the same crime, separated, interrogated, and each offered a deal if they confess. Each is told that, if neither confesses, they'll be convicted and spend a year in jail, while if both confess they'll be convicted on a more serious charge and spend three years in jail. If one confesses and the other stays silent, then the one who confesses gets off free and clear while the other takes the whole rap and spends four years in jail. That's it. The problem for each prisoner is: confess or not? This is summed up in the payoff matrix set out in Table 5.1. Players A and B can each stay silent (cooperate with each other) or confess (defect). There are thus four possible outcomes. The players' payoffs, mostly negative because these are years in jail, are set out in the bottom left corner of each cell for Player A and in the top right corner for Player B.

The PD game has attracted so much attention over the years because it captures a pervasive problem in human interaction. Collectively, the best possible outcome for the prisoners is to stay silent, resulting in two years' jail

Table 5.1 The prisoners' dilemma

		Player B	
		Stay silent (cooperate)	Confess (defect)
Player A	Stay silent (cooperate)	−1 −1	0 −4
	Confess (defect)	−4 0	−3 −3

time between them. However, if one prisoner expects the other to stay silent, it is *very* tempting to confess and get no jail time at all. But both prisoners face the same incentives, and if both confess there is a much worse outcome, individually and collectively; they spend six years in jail between them. If only they could somehow bind themselves to stay silent, then they would both be better off. The trouble is that, absent the possibility of a binding contract between them (and there is nobody to enforce this), both prisoners have a *dominant strategy* to confess. Each is better confessing *whatever the other does*. Prisoner A thinks, "If B stays silent, then I should confess; if B confesses, then I should confess." Prisoner B has exactly the same incentives. The gloomy prediction of the unreconstructed PD game is that both prisoners choose their dominant strategies and confess, resulting in the worst possible collective outcome.

The PD game is important because many significant real-world social interactions, good and bad, seem to have this structure. These include global warming and the pollution of public spaces by dog poop, taxation of multinational corporations, and cellphone pollution in cinemas and theaters. In each case people are collectively better off if they cooperate in the interest of the common good. But they also face huge individual temptations to be selfish and defect, "free riding" by enjoying or exploiting the cooperation of others without contributing to this. Finding ways to solve the prisoner's dilemma has therefore been a longstanding intellectual challenge with great practical significance for public policy. But what has all this to do with ethnocentrism?

Hammond and Axelrod define four different social groups and also four types of agent who differ according to whether, when playing PD games, they cooperate or defect with others from the same, or different, social groups. Table 5.2 describes these types along with their labels in the NetLogo implementation of this model.

Table 5.2 Strategies for playing the PD game, conditional on group membership

	***Cooperate* with opponent of *different* group**	***Defect* with opponent of *different* group**
***Cooperate* with opponent of *same* group**	Altruist (CC)	Ethnocentric (CD)
***Defect* with opponent of *same* group**	Cosmopolitan (DC)	Egoist (DD)

Altruists cooperate unconditionally with others when playing PD games, regardless of social group. Egoists unconditionally defect, using the dominant strategy in the classic PD game regardless of whom they play with. Of special interest are the "ethnocentric" agents, who use a *conditional* decision rule for playing the PD game. They cooperate with people from the same group but defect against members of other groups. The core finding reported by Hammond and Axelrod is that "ethnocentric" agents, defined this particular way, systematically dominate other types of agent in an evolutionary setting, implying that "ethnocentrism pays."

Hammond and Axelrod also define the logical residual category, weirdly called Cosmopolitans in the NetLogo implementation, who defect when playing with people from their own group but cooperate with opponents from other groups. This decision rule seems bizarre and unlikely but is included in the NetLogo model for the sake of completeness. Fortunately, model results imply it is indeed bizarre and unlikely, which is itself a consoling finding.

A NetLogo Model of Ethnocentrism

You will find a faithful replication of Hammond and Axelrod's model of ethnocentrism in the NetLogo models library.[11] In what follows I use a version of the model, **Ethnocentrism 1.0**, which I substantially edited and commented, stripping away redundancies to make the model run faster as well as making the code easier to read. The core model code, however, is elegant and interesting and I have not changed this. As we'll see, my edited code precisely replicates Hammond and Axelrod's published findings.

The environment of the model is the following Prisoners' Dilemma tournament:

- Give agents one of four different colors representing different social groups.
- Give agents a two-feature decision rule for playing PD games. First, do they cooperate (C) or defect (D) with agents from the same group? Second, do they cooperate (C) or defect (D) with agents from different groups?
- Agents therefore have one of four rules for playing PD games, set out in Table 5.2.
- Each iteration, each agent uses its strategy to play a PD game with its four von Neumann neighbors – the four agents touching it vertically or horizontally in the NetLogo world. The payoff for each agent from each game is measured as a change in its probability to reproduce (PTR).

[11] Wilensky, U. 2003. NetLogo Ethnocentrism model. http://ccl.northwestern.edu/netlogo/models/ Ethnocentrism. Center for Connected Learning and Computer-Based Modeling, Northwestern University, Evanston, IL.

- Before each iteration, reset agents' PTRs to a default value that is an important model parameter.
- During each iteration, add agents' positive or negative payoffs from PD games to their PTRs.
- Each iteration involves random death of some agents, random immigration of some new agents, and random agents giving birth to clones, with probability PTR.
- Newborn children are located in an empty von Neumann patch, if one exists, next to their parent; if there is no empty von Neumann patch, there is no birth.
- Newborn children are, with some low probability, mutated from being clones of their parent into different types of agent.
- The whole process is iterated continuously until the observer stops it.

The process set out above generates a *replicator-mutator* evolutionary environment in which more successful types of agent reproduce faster than others and, in some circumstances, may even come to dominate the agent population.

In programming terms, the NetLogo model uses a clever way to implement the continuously iterated multiple PD games that generate this evolutionary tournament. This focuses on the calling agent, who calls its four von Neumann neighbors to play a PD but also gets called to play as a neighbor by every other agent it calls. Each agent is therefore both a giver and a receiver of cooperation and defection in the PD game. Giving cooperation in this model costs −0.01; the receiver of cooperation gets +0.03. Giving defection costs 0; the receiver of defection also gets 0. The net effect for each agent of one iteration of the model is a set of four PD games, each with the payoffs set out in Table 5.3. You can see a difference between the payoffs in Tables 5.3 and 5.1; payoffs in the Hammond-Axelrod ethnocentrism model are all shifted in a positive direction. The *ordering* of payoffs in Table 5.3 is the same as that in Table 5.1, so this is indeed a PD game. What has not been noticed up to now is that, as we soon shall see, the fact that most payoffs in Table 5.3 are positive, not negative, makes

Table 5.3 Payoffs on NetLogo implementation of PD game

	Stay silent (cooperate)	Confess (defect)
Stay silent (cooperate)	−0.01 + 0.03 = **0.02** −0.01 + 0.03 = **0.02**	0 +0.03 = **0.03** −0.01 + 0 = **−0.01**
Confess (defect)	−1+0 = **−0.01** 0 + 0.03 = **3**	0 + 0 = **0** 0 + 0 = **0**

a *big* difference when we dig deeper into the evolutionary environment of the Hammond-Axelrod ethnocentrism model. The payoffs in this model are (positive) probabilities to reproduce, not (negative) years in jail.

Ethnocentrism Model: NetLogo Code

In Appendix 5.1 you'll find **Ethnocentrism 1.0**, my pruned, edited, and recommented version of the original Ethnocentrism model that lives in the NetLogo models library. This gives exactly the same headline result as the model published by Hammond and Axelrod, assuring that my cosmetic surgery has improved general housekeeping, speed, and legibility but not touched the heart of the model. Given all the NetLogo code we discussed in earlier sections of both Elements, I won't take you in detail through the entire model, where you will find extensive comments on each step of the way. I will, however, discuss two key features of this.

The first is the clever way in which the code makes agents play in an iterated PD tournament with their von Neumann neighbors. The second is the model's rudimentary system of setting up replicator-mutator evolutionary dynamics in this tournament. This specifies a simple evolutionary environment in which agents using more successful decision rules prosper relative to those using less successful rules. We will soon see there is a key assumption in the replicator system that turns out to drive almost all of Hammond and Axelrod's reported findings.

The PD tournament between agents is generated by the model's `interact` routine. In this routine each agent interacts with the four others in its von Neumann neighborhood. Commands initiated by `ask turtles-on neighbors4` are interpreted from the perspective of the *agents being asked* – the von Neumann neighbors. To refer back to the *agent doing the asking*, we use the `myself` primitive. Recall the tricky but crucial difference in NetLogo programming between `self` and `myself`. Think of yourself as the person doing the asking. You yourself are `myself` in NetLogo speak. Think of the other agent(s) you are asking to do something as "themselves" or "itself," which NetLogo calls `self`. This is a very common source of errors and crashes. Note that `cooperate-with-same?` and `cooperate-with-different?`, with names ending in ?, are Boolean variables that can be either `true` or `false`.

This code does not, contrary to superficial impressions, result in the game being played twice by a given agent pair. Think of the calling agent as the row player in the PD game in Table 5.3 and each of the four agents on `neighbors4` as column players. Game payoffs arise from a combination of costs of giving and gains from receiving. These are built up in two passes. After the two passes, I have paid any costs of giving and received any gains of receiving. Iterating this code results in each agent playing multiple PD games with its four von Neumann neighbors.

> FIRST PASS: I am the calling agent (row player) and giver. I pay giving costs for each opponent on `neighbors4` who I give to. Each of these receivers (column players) gets the gain of receiving. I pay no giving cost for each opponent I don't give to, and each of these gets zero.

> SECOND PASS: I am one of four opponents (column player) and receiver on `neighbors4` of *another* calling agent. I get the gain of receiving if the calling agent gives to me, and zero if not.

Thus:

```
to interact
    ;; if I cooperate with agents of the same color, reduce my PTR by
    ;; cost-of-giving and increase PTR of neighbors by gain of receiving
ask turtles-on neighbors4 [

  if color = [color] of myself
    [if [cooperate-with-same?] of myself [
        ask myself [ set PTR PTR - cost-of-giving ]     ;; I pay
        set PTR PTR + gain-of-receiving]]               ;; neighbors4 gain

    ;; Note the nested "ifs". Payoffs only distributed above if my
    ;; neighbor is same color AND I cooperate with same, else zero
    ;; Similarly, if we are different colors, if I cooperate with agents
    ;; of different color I reduce my PTR and reward my neighbors

if color != [color] of myself [

  if [cooperate-with-different?] of myself [
    ask myself [ set PTR PTR - cost-of-giving ]
    set PTR PTR + gain-of-receiving]]

]
    ;; The net effect after all interactions is a PD game with the
    ;; mutual defection PTR payoff normalized to zero
end
```

The replicator-mutator dynamics of the model is set up by its `death`, `immigrate`, `reproduce`, and `mutate` procedures. The `death` procedure creates turnover of agents each iteration by killing agents with probability `death-rate`. This is an important model parameter set on the interface, defaulting to a high value of 0.10 in Hammond and Axelrod's published work. (Ten percent of the population is killed every iteration!) Unlike more sophisticated evolutionary models, agent death is completely random and does not depend on agents' fitness, that is, on how successful they have been in the past. We can easily modify the baseline model to take account of this although, as I note below, I tried this and it doesn't make much difference to model output. So leave things as they are in the baseline model to keep things simple.

The immigrate procedure causes new agents, immigrants, to enter the world on random empty patches. Each immigrant has a randomly chosen one of the four possible groups and a randomly chosen one of the four possible strategies.

The heart of the evolutionary dynamics in this model is in the repro-duce procedure, which uses each agent's postgame probability-to-reproduce (PTR) to determine if it gets to reproduce. The more success-fully the agent played its PD games in the most recent model cycle, the more likely it is to reproduce. A very restrictive key feature of reproduc-tion as modeled by Hammond and Axelrod, which as we will see drives most of their results, is that children can only be located in one of the parent's four von Neumann patches, so that an agent can reproduce only if one of these patches is empty, that is: with [not any? turtles-here].

```
to reproduce
  if random-float 1.0 < PTR [
    let destination one-of neighbors4 with [not any? turtles-here]
    if destination != nobody [
                ;; Agent can only reproduce if a von Neumann patch is empty
      hatch 1 [
                ;; Hatch a clone of the current turtle in the new location
        move-to destination
        mutate        ;; then mutate the clone/child
    ]]]
end
```

Once they have been generated, new clones are subjected to mutation with some small probability, determined by the mutation-rate, another impor-tant model parameter. This is the mutator part of the replicator-mutator system.

```
to mutate
  if random-float 1.0 < mutation-rate [   ;; first mutate the color
    let old-color color
    while [color = old-color]
      [ set color random-color ]]
            ;; MAKE the color change; NB not just give it a chance to change
            ;; now mutate the strategy variables, using NOT to toggle them
  if random-float 1.0 < mutation-rate [
    set cooperate-with-same? not cooperate-with-same?]
  if random-float 1.0 < mutation-rate [
    set cooperate-with-different? not cooperate-with-different?]
  update-shape      ;; the agent's shape reflects its strategy
end
```

Model Burn-in

Hammond and Axelrod use what they call a "standard" run length of 2,000 iterations, though they never discuss any burn-in diagnostics that lead them to this conclusion. They do, however, report a result relevant to burn-in: when they shortened the model run to 500 iterations, the evolved percentage of ethnocentric agents was significantly lower. This implies their model was *not* burnt-in at 500 iterations. Figure 5.1 shows burn-in diagnostics for the baseline Hammond-Axelrod model, based on eight very long (20,000-iteration) run repetitions, generated by experiment 1 of the model **Ethnocentrism 1.0**. (Recall that we use eight diagnostic repetitions because this is an efficient use of an eight-core machine.)

I move the discussion of model burn-in back from appendices to the main text because establishing the burn-in era for evolutionary models is more challenging. Different model outputs may well converge at different rates, but our main quantity of interest here is in the evolved proportion of "ethnocentric" agents. The diagnostic plots in Figure 5.1 focus on this. Presenting things somewhat differently from previous sections, I superimpose results from each run repetition, plotted in different colors, on the same plot. This shows the evolved proportion of ethnocentric agents, those using the CD strategy. The top panel shows that this evidently converges on a stochastic steady state for each repetition. The bottom panel of Figure 5.1, showing the first 1,500 iterations of each repetition, suggests it is safe to assume convergence (with this model parametrization) after 1,000 iterations. We also see clearly from this plot why Hammond and Axelrod found that the proportion of ethnocentric agents was still evolving after 500 iterations.

Baseline Results

Hammond and Axelrod report the mean proportion of ethnocentric agents over the final 100 iterations of 2,000-iteration run repetitions, giving no justification for choosing 100 iterations. The top panel of Figure 5.2 reports box plots of the mean proportion of ethnocentric agents over the final 200 iterations of the eight very long (20,000-iteration) burnt-in diagnostic repetitions and shows there is still considerable variation in these. The box in box plots represent the middle 50 percent of observations, the 25th to 75th percentile, and the line in the middle of this box shows the median observation. There is clearly a need to conduct multiple repetitions with the same parameterization and aggregate results from these. The bottom panel confirms this, reporting mean proportions of ethnocentric agents over the entire 19,000 burnt-in iterations of the long diagnostic repetitions. We still see significant variation in the medians of our main quantity of interest, the mean proportion of ethnocentric agents, showing that there is

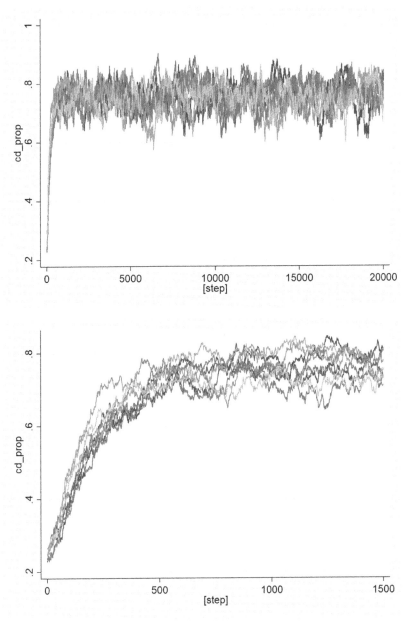

Figure 5.1 Evolving proportion of ethnocentric agents during eight long
diagnostic repetitions

some residual path dependence in key model outputs. In what follows, therefore, we treat each run repetition as burnt-in "fit for purpose" at 1,000 iterations
and estimate quantities of interest using multiple burnt-in repetitions.

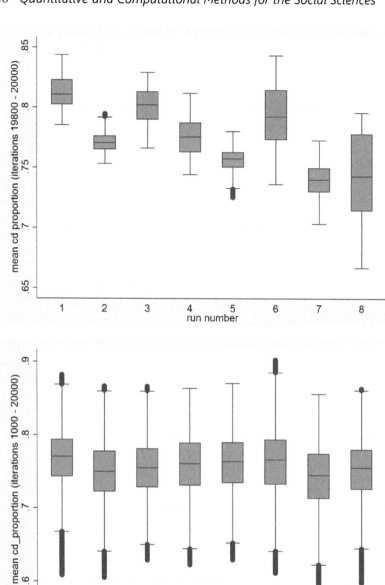

Figure 5.2 Mean proportion of ethnocentric agents over the final 100 (top panel) and 19,000 (bottom panel) iterations of eight long repetitions

We can also use results of these diagnostic run repetitions to check Hammond and Axelrod's headline published finding, which was that the evolved proportion of ethnocentric agents (CD) was 0.76, as opposed to the figure of 0.25 we would find if the four different strategies were equally successful. This is the key simulation result Hammond and Axelrod use to support the claim that "ethnocentrism" pays. Averaging results from iterations 1901 to 2000 in the eight repetitions to replicate precisely what Hammond and Axelrod did, we find the proportion of ethnocentric agents to be 0.76, perfectly replicating their published findings. This is reassuring, though note that this figure varied between 0.73 and 0.81 across the eight repetitions, so model output remains path-dependent. We found the mean proportion over eight repetitions of altruistic agents, who cooperate unconditionally (CC), to be 0.14. The mean proportion of egoistic agents, who never cooperate (DD), was 0.08. Only 2 percent of agents on average were in the weird residual category of agents who only cooperate with others who are *not* like them (DC). One possible explanation for why there *any* agents of this type at all is that these were immigrant agents randomly given this decision rule, but with almost no long-term prospect of survival.

Stress-Testing the Finding That "Ethnocentrism Pays"

I interrogated agent-based models in previous sections by systematically varying key model parameters. I do things differently here, building on work by Andrew Bausch, who showed that the key Hammond-Axelrod finding on ethnocentrism is brittle, disappearing completely in the face of small but plausible changes in key modeling assumptions.[12] Briefly, Bausch begins by showing that "ethnocentrism" continues to pay according to this model *even when there is only one social group* – showing that something peculiar is going on, since ethnocentrism has absolutely no meaning in this context. He then shows how two modeling assumptions make this happen. The first is that offspring can only be born on and reside in patches that are von Neumann neighbors of the reproducing agent. The second is that agents can interact only with others who are their von Neumann neighbors. The net effect is that the model world evolves into a state in which agents typically interact only with their own offspring, who are clones of themselves (subject to a tiny mutation probability). It is this hyperlocal and incestuous reproduction and interaction that drives the influential Hammond-Axelrod finding, not "ethnocentrism" per se in the sense of defecting, regardless of location, against members of other groups and cooperating with members of your own group.

Andrew Bausch does a lot of careful work to show this, but here I make three rough and ready modifications to the model so we can quickly see what is going on. I edit the baseline model in three different and very basic ways to allow the following: only one social group, not four; offspring to reside on *any* empty

---

[12] Bausch, A. W. 2015. The Geography of Ethnocentrism. *Journal of Conflict Resolution*, *59*(3), 510–527.

patch in the NetLogo world, not just empty von Neumann patches (if these exist); agents to interact with *any* other agent, not just von Neumann neighbors.

However, I conclude by showing that, if we do nonetheless accept that the hyperlocal reproduction and interaction implied by the baseline Hammond-Axelrod model really is part of what we commonly understand by ethnocentrism, then we can investigate the evolutionary environment to show something much more interesting and suggestive than has been shown in previous published work. Starting with an agent population *comprising only unconditional defectors* but allowing for immigration and random mutation of agent strategies at the point of reproduction, I show that the ethnocentric strategy can evolve, as if from nowhere, to dominate the NetLogo world.

One Social Group

It's easy to modify the Hammond-Axelrod model to comprehend only one social group rather than four. Go to the `create-turtle` procedure and change `set color random-color` to `set color red`. Delete the `ran-dom-color` procedure. Delete everything associated with the first `if` instruction in the `mutate` procedure, since this mutates the new agent's `color`. You now have a one-group model, **Ethnocentrism 1.1** one group, in which some agents nonetheless deploy "ethnocentric" decision rules.

Figure 5.3 shows the evolving proportion of "ethnocentric" agents in this one-group world, keeping all other model parameters exactly the same as in the baseline model and repeating the eight very long run repetitions. This was experiment 2 of the **model Ethnocentrism 1.1**.

The evolved proportion of "ethnocentric" agents in stochastic steady state is 0.41. This proportion is not as high as when there are four groups but is substantially higher than the 0.25 we would observe if agents chose their decision rule at random. "Ethnocentrism" pays *even in settings where it is completely redundant,* since ethnocentric agents never encounter an agent from a different group against whom they can defect! What is going on?

The answer lurks in the baseline model's assumption of hyperlocal agent reproduction and interaction, which confines these key activities to agents' von Neumann neighbors. When agents reproduce they put *clones* of themselves onto their von Neumann patches, the four patches vertically or horizontally touching them, *provided one of these is empty.* These clones are then subject to a tiny probability of mutation. As `death` randomly culls each agent's von Neumann neighbors these are replaced with offspring who are *almost always its clones.* And since interaction is also confined by assumption to von Neumann neighbors, the world evolves to a state in which *agents' interactions are almost*

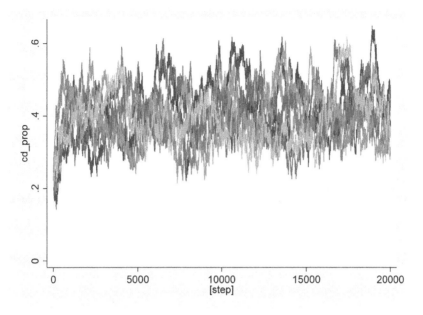

Figure 5.3 Evolving proportion of "ethnocentric" agents during eight long repetitions when there is only one social group

always with clones of themselves – coming from the same social group and using the same conditional decision rule when playing the PD.

We don't need a simulation to tell us that, when two clones from the same social group and using the CD rule play a PD game against each other, the outcome will be mutual cooperation resulting in the highest possible joint payoff in terms of enhanced reproductive fitness. The CD rule works very well, by construction resulting in mutual cooperation, *when played against other agents from the same group who also play CD*. Its great weakness is that it performs very badly against agents from the same group using DD, unconditional defection. Same-group interactions between CD and DD result in a maximal loss for the agent using CD and a maximal gain for agent using DD. *That* after all, is the whole point of the Prisoners' Dilemma! The DD player exploits the CD player. The CD rule is very costly whenever used against DD, but this almost never happens in the Hammond-Axelrod Ethnocentrism model. This is because, as we just saw, CD players are insulated against the possibility of playing against DD players by a hyperlocal environment for reproduction and interaction that leaves them almost always playing against clones of themselves.

Exactly the same argument applies to the CC rule, which should be equally effective when used in interactions with same-group clones – and equally disastrous when deployed against agents using DD. In a one-group world where agents never meet others from a different group, only the first feature of their decision rule – the first C in CC and CD – is relevant. The second feature is redundant, since it deals with interactions with agents from other groups, which never happen. We therefore expect that evolved proportions of CC agents will be the same as for CD agents in a one-group world. Indeed, an identical plot to Figure 5.3 can be drawn for CC agents, the evolved proportion of which was also 0.41. Expressed in evolutionary terms, we can think of the "D" in the CD rule when there is only one group as equivalent to *noncoding* (redundant) DNA. It serves no useful function but passes from generation to generation because it does no harm. And as we will see at the end of this section, it does play a latent defensive role against some future invasion of the environment by agents belonging to different groups and/or using different decision rules.

Alerted by all this to the effects of assuming hyperlocal and incestuous environments for social interaction, we now dig deeper by making two simple modifications to the baseline ethnocentrism model. The first tells reproducing agents to locate their offspring on *any* empty patch in the NetLogo world, not only on their von Neumann neighbors. The second tells agents to interact with four random agents located *anywhere* in the NetLogo world, not only with von Neumann neighbors.

Babies Everywhere

Changing the baseline ethnocentrism model to instruct reproducing agents to locate their offspring on *any* vacant patch is very simple. In the `reproduce` procedure, just replace one word, turning:

```
let destination one-of neighbors4 with [not any? turtles-here]
```
   into:
```
let destination one-of patches with [not any? turtles-here].
```

Everything else stays the same in the resulting model, **Ethnocentrism 1.2 babies everywhere**. However, changing a single word in the code generates a *very* different structure of social interaction and *radically* changes the theoretical inferences we draw from the model. Figure 5.4 shows results derived from the first 1,500 cycles of eight 20,000-cycle run repetitions, now locating the offspring of reproducing agents anywhere in the NetLogo world but leaving every other parameter the same as for the baseline model. This was experiment 3 of the model **Ethnocentrism 1.2**. These repetitions look burnt-in at around 750 cycles.

The startling difference with Figure 5.1, however, is that *we are now plotting the proportion of egoistic agents*, using the DD decision rule. This rule unconditionally defects against all comers and is the dominant strategy in the unreconstructed PD game. Averaging the proportions of agents using each decision rule over the

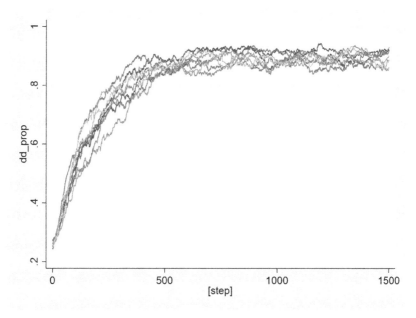

Figure 5.4 Evolving proportion of egoistic (DD) agents during eight long repetitions in which offspring can locate on any vacant patch

final 19,000 cycles of the eight 20,000-cycle repetitions, we find that 89 percent of agents use DD, 8 percent use CD, 3 percent use DC, and 1 percent use CC.

In short, the "ethnocentrism pays" argument *collapses completely* when we remove the assumption of hyperlocal *reproduction*. What pays in this new setting is the traditional dominant strategy for the PD game of unconditional defection, which evolves to dominate the model world. As we will soon see, the fact that any agent at all still uses a non-DD rule is largely a function of ongoing random mutations and regular invasions by agents using randomly chosen rules. Indeed, given these mutations and invasions, the long-term robustness of the dominant PD strategy, DD, is impressive.

Opponents Anywhere

Another simple change in the baseline model is to remove the assumption of hyperlocal *interaction*, telling agents to interact with four randomly chosen opponents located anywhere in the NetLogo world. This super-easy fix changes the `interact` procedure as follows: Delete

```
ask turtles-on neighbors4 [...
```

and replace with

```
let opponents n-of 4 other turtles
ask opponents [...
```

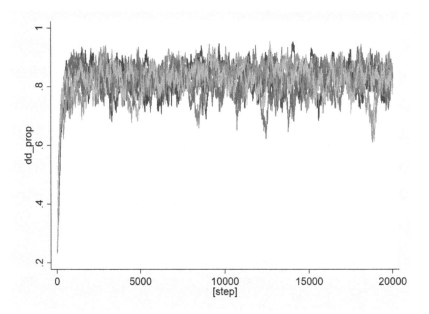

Figure 5.5 Evolving proportion of egoistic (DD) agents during eight long repetitions in which agents pick four random PD opponents located anywhere in the NetLogo world

Nothing else changes. The result is the model **Ethnocentrism 1.3 opponents anywhere**. Figure 5.5 shows the evolving proportion of egoistic (DD) agents during eight 20,000-cycle model run repetitions using the new rule for choosing others to interact with in the PD game, but leaving every other parameter the same as for the baseline model. This is experiment 5 in the model **Ethnocentrism 1.3**. Averaging proportions of agents using each decision rule over the final 19,000 cycles of the 20,000-cycle repetitions, we find that 83 percent use DD, 12 percent use CD, 3 percent use DC, and 1 percent use CC. The "ethnocentrism pays" argument again *collapses completely*, this time when we remove the assumption of hyperlocal *interaction*. Once more, what pays in this setting is DD, the traditional dominant strategy of unconditional defection in the PD game.

Check for yourself what happens if you modify the baseline ethnocentrism model to delete *both* hyperlocal reproduction *and* hyperlocal interaction at the same time!

Sustainability of a World Populated Only by Egoists

This, however, is far from the end of the story. We now turn to another key assumption lurking in the out-of-the-box ethnocentrism model, which has to do with the relationship between default settings of several model parameters:

those generating the payoffs in the PD game, the death rate, and the baseline probability (PTR) for each agent to reproduce.

The default parametrization of this ethnocentrism model normalizes the mutual PD defection payoff to zero, recalling that this payoff is a change in the agent's probability to reproduce (PTR). This normalization has a huge effect, since the default death rate is set at 0.10 and the default PTR at 0.12. All of this means that, in a world populated solely by egoists playing DD, their baseline PTR remains at 0.12 after their zero PD payoff for mutual defection, in the face of a death rate of 0.10. The evolutionary environment set up in this way is not punishing the population of egoists for their lack of cooperation by driving their reproduction rate below the death rate. This makes it possible to sustain a world comprising only egoists. *But this default parametrization is completely arbitrary*! It relies on no information gleaned from the real world, whether about the baseline death rate, the baseline payoff for mutual defection, or the baseline probability to reproduce. The person who coded the model picked these numbers for some reason or another but did not share this reason with others. And the numbers that were picked make a *big* difference. As we will now see, these particular numbers, picked without any justification, completely drive the influential published result.

The parameterization of the PD game for the baseline ethnocentrism model is at odds with most interpretations of the PD as modeling a real, substantive problem in human social interaction, in which mutual defection has a *negative* payoff. The defecting prisoners both go to jail; polluters destroy their own environment. The underlying assumption in this general theoretical account is that some element of repeated mutual cooperation is essential to the prosperity and survival of large populations – that widespread and repeated mutual defection destroys value and generates an existential threat to the population as a whole. This is the "tragedy of the commons," or indeed the problem of global warming.

The baseline ethnocentrism model, by normalizing the mutual defection payoff to zero and adjusting other payoffs to have the same rank order, does not change the structure of the PD *in a one-shot game*. What Hammond and Axelrod and subsequent scholars seem to have overlooked, however, is that this makes a *big* difference when we iterate the game in an evolutionary setting. This is because the zero payoff for mutual defection does *not* make widespread and repeated mutual defection an existential threat to the population of agents.

We can easily change game parameters to generate a negative agent payoff for mutual defection. Simply lower the baseline PTR from 0.12 to 0.09, noting that neither number is calibrated in any way to social interactions in the real world, so each is as good as the other in this sense. The PD game is *exactly the*

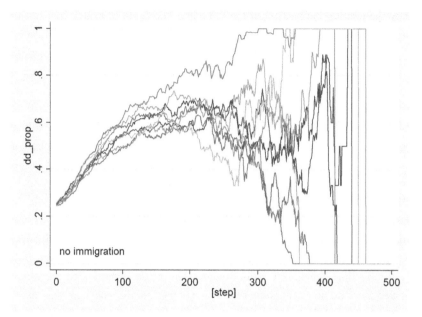

Figure 5.6 Evolving proportion of egoistic (DD) agents when offspring can locate on any vacant patch, with payoff for mutual defection (0.09) below death rate (0.10) and zero immigration

same but, in a replicator-mutator evolutionary environment, there is a very different *effect* on the evolution of large populations if we lower the baseline probability to reproduce below the death rate. As shown by the PD payoffs set out in Table 5.3, mutual defection results in a zero increase in PTR for defecting agents, now leaving them with a default probability to reproduce of 0.09 but facing a death rate of 0.10. The –0.01 "sucker" payoff for cooperating with a defector now takes aggregate PTR payoffs for suckers well below the death rate. The 0.02 per game payoff rewards agents for mutual cooperation by taking their PTR over the death rate. Finally, the highest PTR payoff is still reserved for egoists who can find cooperating suckers to play with.

Make this simple parameter change to the baseline model, lowering `initial-PTR` to 0.09. For reasons to which we shortly return, turn off immigration of new agents by setting the `immigration-per-day` to 0. You need no new model code to do this and can make both changes on the model's interface. Using this parameterization, rerun the **Ethnocentrism 1.2** babies everywhere version of the model, which resulted in the dominance of egoists playing DD, reported in Figure 5.4. Figure 5.6 shows the very striking results of eight long run repetitions, focusing on the early stages, where all the action takes place. You see an initial explosion in the proportion of egoists until they dominate the population, followed by *total extinction of the agent popula-tion in less than 500 iterations*! This is precisely the tragedy of the commons. We're now pushing this model *far* beyond its well-known published findings. You might think Figure 5.6 looks a little messy. Wearing my theorist's hat, however, I see it as a really beautiful summary of the evolution of the canonical collective action problem.

This ecological collapse happens because the evolutionary success of the dominant DD strategy now requires positive PD payoffs if egoists are to reproduce. Using the DD strategy against other agents who defect now gives a negative payoff, measured in probability to reproduce, as in the classic PD story. The survival of *a population of agents using DD* now depends critically on the continued existence of other agents using decision rules involving cooperation. This cooperation by others can then be exploited by egoists, who defect unconditionally, turn cooperating agents into suckers, and earn the positive evolutionary payoff that comes from defecting against a cooperating sucker. The other types of agent in effect serve as prey for the egoists. However, the more successful the egoists are, the less successful their prey, whose numbers consequently decline in an evolutionary setting. Once the egoists become completely dominant, there are too few prey agents for them to exploit. This is a classic predator-prey problem in evolutionary dynamics. The popula-tion of egoists suffers a total evolutionary collapse, just as any predator popula-tion collapses if it eradicates its prey, and just as in the tragedy of the commons. This is an important new finding from the model: *a mix of agents using other decision rules is necessary for the evolutionary survival of a subpopulation of egoists*.

How, then, does the dominant population of egoists shown in Figures 5.4 and 5.5 sustain itself? The simple answer to this question has hardly been discussed but is a core feature of the Hammond-Axelrod model of ethnocentrism. This is *immigration*. Immigrants in this model provide a constant influx of new agents who have random group membership and a decision rule chosen randomly from four possibilities in the rule set. If other agents are potential suckers who can be exploited by egoists, then immigration provides a continuous inflow of suckers. This allows a population comprising mainly egoists to survive and avert the inexorable slide toward extinction, which occurs when there is no inflow of immigrants and the egoists have consumed the subpopulation of existing suckers.

Figure 5.7 reports results of a Behavior Space experiment that reruns the baseline ethnocentrism model but changes the default parameterization to make PTR = 0.09 as in Figure 5.6 and varies the immigration rate from 2/day to 40/day in increments of 2. There were eight 1,000-cycle repetitions

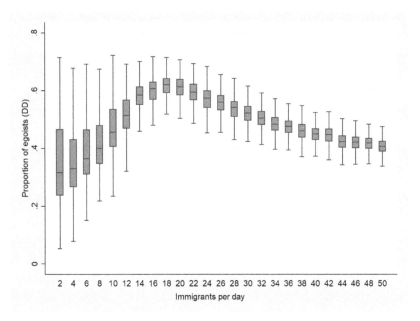

Figure 5.7 Evolved proportion of egoistic (DD) agents, by immigration rate, when offspring can locate on any vacant patch, with payoff for mutual defection (0.09) below death rate (0.10)

per parameter setting. This is experiment 6 in the **Ethnocentrism 1.2** model. We see a box plot of the proportions of egoists during the final 500 cycles of each run – by which time, as Figure 5.6 clearly shows, the agent population would have been extinct without immigration. The inflow of immigrants prevents the agent population from becoming extinct, even if most agents unconditionally defect when playing PD games with others. Increasing the flow of immigrants, who can be exploited by the egoists, has a strikingly nonlinear effect, as we expect theoretically with predator-prey evolutionary dynamics. Initially, having more immigrants is associated with increasing prosperity for egoists, who thrive by exploiting the increasing supply of immigrant suckers. A sweet spot for the egoists arises at an immigration rate of about 18–20/day in the terms of this model, after which the proportion of egoists goes into a steady decline. This is likely because an increasing proportion of the surviving population are immigrants, who have only a 25 percent chance of being egoists. The best situation *for the subpopulation of egoists*, it seems from this, is that there be enough cooperating immigrants for them to exploit as suckers but not so many that immigrants begin to dominate the population.

Emergence of "Ethnocentrism"

I now turn to another striking finding that to my knowledge has not been reported before. First, let's accept the *very* restrictive definition of ethnocentrism implicit in the Hammond-Axelrod model. This involves a PD decision rule of "cooperate with same but defect against others." But it also involves hyperlocal reproduction, according to which offspring are almost always clones and must also be immediate neighbors. And it involves hyperlocal interaction according to which the PD games can only be played with immediate neighbors, who as we have seen are typically clones. Given this very particular definition of ethnocentrism, I now show that ethnocentric decision rules can emerge *even from a population in which there are no ethnocentric agents at all*. If we do indeed accept the restrictive hyperlocal definition of ethnocentrism, this is a *much* stronger finding than the well-known published results.

As always, changes to the NetLogo model needed to implement this are very simple. What we want to do is to take the baseline model and change the setup procedure so that, at the start of each model run, all agents are unconditional defectors (DD) or, alternatively, all agents are unconditional cooperators (CC). To achieve this, edit the baseline setup procedure and add two more procedures before the create-turtle procedure. Add a switch to the interface that sets a new Boolean global variable, DD-start? to either true or false. If true, all agents begin playing DD; if false, all agents begin playing CC. Everything else stays exactly the same. Thus:

```
to setup
  ca
  ask patches [ifelse DD-start?
            [create-defectors ] [create-cooperators]]
  reset-ticks
end

to create-defectors
  sprout 1 [
    set color random-color
    set cooperate-with-same? false
    set cooperate-with-different? false
    update-shape
  ]
end

to create-cooperators
    sprout 1 [
    set color random-color
    set cooperate-with-same? true
    set cooperate-with-different? true
```

```
    update-shape
  ]
end
```

This gives us a *starting* population of agents who belong to random groups (colors), but who are all egoists if DD-start? is true; else they are all altruists. However, *immigrant* agents created during a model run are still initiated by the original create-turtle procedure, which gives them a random color and *a decision rule picked randomly from the full rule set* (DD, CC, CD, DC). Meanwhile, the decision rules of reproducing offspring are still subject to mutation into one of the full rule set. The resulting model is **Ethnocentrism 1.4 CD evolves**.

Starting from a population consisting entirely of egoists (DD) or entirely of altruists (CC) with no ethnocentric agent at all, the theoretically interesting open question is whether the processes of immigration and mutation allow the ethnocentric decision rule (CD) not only to establish itself but to become dominant.

We answer this question with a Behavior Space experiment involving eight 2,000-cycle run repetitions with the default model parameterization but DD-start? == false, and eight otherwise identical repetitions with DD-start? == true. This is experiment 8 of the model **Ethnocentrism 1.4** (experiment 7 performs burn-in diagnostics for the revised model). The results, reported in Figure 5.8, are both striking and consistent, suggesting that the sets of eight 2,000-cycle repetitions are sufficient to establish a clear pattern. Figure 5.8 plots the evolving proportion of ethnocentric agents (CD) in red for each set of simulations. The relative success of the CC (top panel) and DD (bottom panel) rules are plotted in green and black respectively and are of great theoretical and substantive interest.

In each case, *starting with no ethnocentric agents whatsoever*, the twin processes of immigration and mutation not only introduce the ethnocentric decision rule into the agent population but allow it quickly (by about 500 model cycles) to become dominant. This holds whether the starting population is all altruist or all egoist. What this suggests is that, given hyperlocal reproduction and interaction, the evolutionary processes modeled here, involving immigration and the mutation of a very small proportion of offspring, are likely to lead to ethnocentric behaviors, *even when none previously existed*. This seems (to me) to be *much* more interesting and important than the published Hammond-Axelrod finding about ethnocentrism. Always accepting this very restrictive definition of ethnocentrism, the CD decision rule for playing PD games is a successful invasive species in this evolutionary environment.

Conclusions

This simple model of "ethnocentrism" gives us a lot to think about. The most important thing is that attaching a real-world name to a theoretical model does not

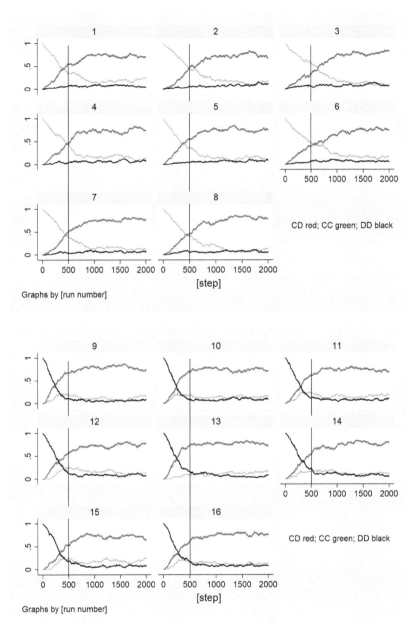

Figure 5.8 Evolving proportions of agents using different decision rules starting from a population comprised entirely of altruists (top panel) or of egoists (bottom panel).

make it a model of the real world. I can call some model "democracy", but its name does not itself make it a model of a real democracy. I've put "ethnocentrism" in quotes throughout this section because, while the NetLogo model is *called* Ethnocentrism, we've seen clearly that the superficially plausible "cooperate with same, defect against others" "ethnocentric" decision rule is not the main reason why ethnocentric agents tend to prevail according to the model. Lurking in the model code are two additional conditions, hyperlocal reproduction and hyperlocal interaction, which are necessary for "ethnocentric" behaviors to succeed. If either one of these two necessary conditions is subtracted, the model's published and theoretically influential results on "ethnocentrism" vanish entirely.

This lesson applies more generally – not only to other models in these Elements but to all models. In this case, we're *not* saying that the baseline model is wrong. What we *are* saying is that we must be careful to *confine our claims about a theoretical model's implications for some feature of the real world to the detailed implementation of this feature in the model*. If you take only one lesson from what we have been doing in these Elements, that's the lesson. It's a lesson that applies *to any abstract model of the real world* and is not in the least confined to computational modeling.

A second important new feature of the model in this section is its tournament design. For the first time in these Elements, we compared the effectiveness of different decision rules that agents might use – in this case four different rules for playing multiple Prisoners' Dilemma games (CC, CD, DC, DD) in an environment where agents may belong to different social groups. The tournament makes agents repeatedly play PD games with others who may or may not use the same decision rule. The aim is to find out which rule is most effective in this setting. Do agents using one particular rule (CD in this case) systematically perform better than others?

More generally, the tournament is an important device in agent-based modeling because we do think it very realistic to assume that agents *do not all use the same decision rule,* that different people try to solve the same problem in different ways. This means we are interested in whether agents who use one type of decision rule systematically tend to outperform others. The published tournament result that motivated this section, radically qualified in the course of the section, was that agents using the CD rule in this setting systematically tend to prosper. You may well find other tournaments very useful in developing your own ideas, and we can also think about how tournaments could be bolted on to the other models investigated in these Elements.

Related to this, a third feature of the model's results when different agents use different decision rules, graphically illustrated in Figures 5.6 and 5.7, is that a stochastic steady state may involve a *mix of agents using different decision rules*. In this case we saw that the survival of a subpopulation of egoists, who unconditionally defect when playing PD games, may depend on the continuing survival of subpopulations of more cooperative agents, who can be exploited by egoists. This is another general feature of agent-based models, once we take account of the fact that in the real world different people often do attack the same problem in different ways. One of the nice things about agent-based modeling more generally is that it is well suited to investigating the *stable coexistence, and indeed symbiosis, of very different types of agent* – something we routinely observe in the real world.

This conclusion depends upon another important new device in agent-based modeling introduced in this section: a rudimentary evolutionary environment. Some agents die after each iteration, though in this model they die randomly, not as a function of either their age or their evolutionary fitness. It is as if all agents have identical fitness and could in theory live forever but are killed by random bolts from the blue. Agents also have the opportunity each iteration to reproduce. Central to the Hammond-Axelrod model, their probability of reproducing is conditional on their success at playing PD games in the previous iteration, which we can think of as a form of evolutionary fitness. More successful agents reproduce more rapidly, allowing us to make inferences about the relative effectiveness of different decision rules from the evolved relative proportions of agents using these rules.

While we can think of many improvements to this simple evolutionary environment, it does still enable the evolution of proportions of agents using different decision rules into a stochastic steady state, allowing us to draw reliable conclusions about the relative success of each decision rule. Going beyond this, our final experiment on the emergence of ethnocentrism from a population comprising only egoists, accepting the baseline model's very restrictive specification of ethnocentrism, is both highly suggestive and a clear illustration of the value of evolutionary modeling.

There are simple ways to make the evolutionary environment better, although in this case they do not much affect the findings we derive from the model. For example, we could easily condition the `death-rate` for each agent on its success at playing PD games. To do this, delete the `death-rate` global slider from the interface and declare `death-rate` as an agent variable by adding it to the `turtles-own` command. Referring back to Table 5.3, we see that mutually cooperating agents get 0.02 added to their PTR for each PD they play, making 0.08 for a cycle of four games played with von Neumann neighbors. Given a default PTR of 0.12, an agent with four consummated mutual coopera-tions will end up with a PTR of 0.20. In the `death` procedure, ask agents to set `death-rate 0.20` – PTR then if `random-float 1.0 < death-rate [die]`. This means that mutual cooperators have a zero `death-rate` and mutual defectors a `death-rate` of 0.08. We've now conditioned agents' death-rates on their PD payoffs. If you try running experiments with this model (and I've done this, though for the sake of clarity I don't report the results here), you'll find essentially the same results as with the simpler evolutionary model, though patterns evolve more quickly. The model looks more evolutionary, but the results are in effect the same. I tried various other refinements to the evolutionary environment of this model with essentially the same effect – somewhat faster evolution but no substantially different results. Given this, there is no huge reason to replace the simpler published model with a fancier alternative that does not affect headline conclusions.

More generally, rigorous evolutionary modeling using classical analytical techniques is rightly seen as very hard and esoteric – the preserve of a select few highly talented theorists. But we have just seen that it is not in the least hard to program and then analyze a simple evolutionary environment in an agent-based model. This is a great example of how agent-based modeling can bring real analytical firepower, once confined to the penthouse of the ivory tower, right down to street level. What I find so exciting is that this lets you focus on the *substance* of the social interactions that really interest you, without worrying about whether the resulting puzzles will be too difficult for you to solve.

In this section, we in effect coded each agent's DNA as a two-position string that can have either C or D in either position, giving four species of agent: CC, CD, DC, DD. For more complicated examples, we can extend this string to have many more positions, each position representing some feature of an agent's decision rule. For example: am I a risk taker or not; am I greedy, wanting my payoffs now, or patient, willing to wait; how deeply do I consider how *you* might respond to my actions; do I condition my actions on any number of features of the environment. It's not at all hard in an agent-based model to extend the string of decision rule DNA by adding very plausible features. And it's not at all hard to investigate all this in the type of evolutionary environment used in this section.

We concluded the previous Element with the lesson that making ABMs more realistic is a simple matter of adding additional realistic features – but that this may well harm intuition by making the model much more complex, so its workings become much harder to understand. The same lesson holds here. We should be excited by the prospect of easily specifying a model world in which a large number of different but realistic types of agent coevolve together. I myself certainly find this very exciting to think about. But the price we will pay for this added realism will be a complex evolutionary model that is easy to code and run but hard to understand. By all means be ambitious and take steps in this direction, but take small and simple steps and think about them carefully as you move forward.

Appendix 3.1

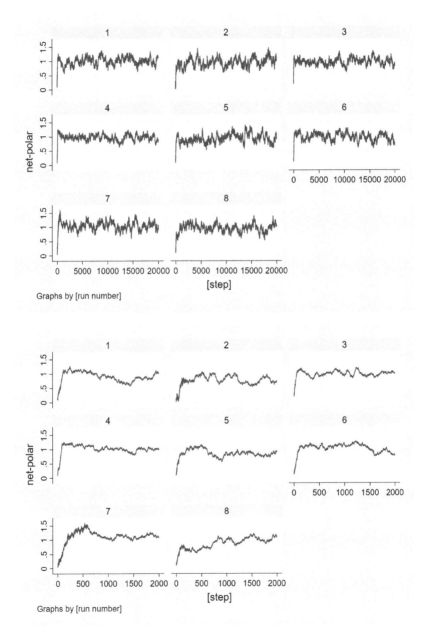

Figure A3.1 Random network model burn-in. 20,000 cycles (top panel), 2,000 cycles (bottom panel)

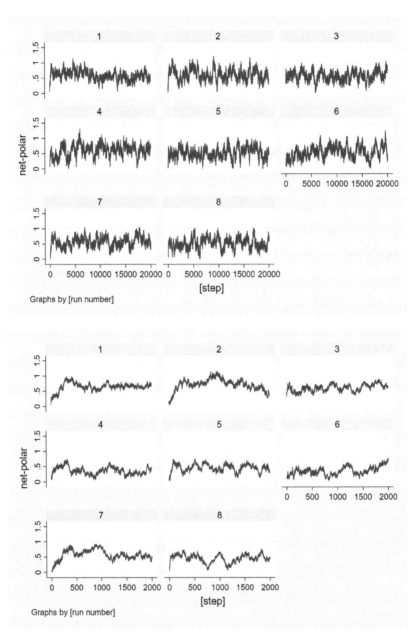

Figure A3.2 Preferential attachment network model burn-in. 20,000 cycles (top panel), 2,000 cycles (bottom panel)

Appendix 4.1
NetLogo Code for XC Model

```
;;_____
;;
;; SETUP AND HOUSEKEEPING
;;_____

breed [citizens citizen]      ; citizens have endogenous ideal points
breed [hardliners hardliner]  ; hardliners do not

globals [
a0 a1                         ; n of agents with position 0 or 1 on cleavage a
b0 b1                         ; n of agents with position 0 or 1 on cleavage b
]

turtles-own [
cleavage-a cleavage-b         ; agent's group on cleavages a and b
subgroup                      ; agent's 2 x 2 subgroup
peer                          ; "who" of agent identified as peer
]

to setup
   clear-all
   ask patches [set pcolor white]
   create-citizens n-pop [setxy random-xcor random-ycor]

   ;; assign agents to categories 0 or 1 on cleavages a and b
   ;; proportions in each category on each cleavage read from the interface
   ;; xc, set on the interface, is the association between cleavage positions
   ;; xc = 0, perfect reinforcing; xc = 0.5, maximum cross-cutting

   set a0 round (cleavage-a-mean * n-pop)
   set a1 n-pop - a0
   set b0 round (cleavage-b-mean * n-pop)
   set b1 n-pop - b0

   ask citizens [set cleavage-a 0]
   ask n-of a1 citizens [set cleavage-a 1]

   ask citizens with [cleavage-a = 0] [set cleavage-b 0]
   ask n-of (a0 * xc) citizens with [cleavage-a = 0] [set cleavage-b 1]
   ask citizens with [cleavage-a = 1] [set cleavage-b 1]
   ask n-of (a1 * xc) citizens with [cleavage-a = 1] [set cleavage-b 0]
```

```
; assign subgroups and colors
ask citizens [
               if (cleavage-a = 1 and cleavage-b = 1) [set subgroup 11
                set color blue]
               if (cleavage-a = 1 and cleavage-b = 0) [set subgroup 10
                set color cyan]
               if (cleavage-a = 0 and cleavage-b = 1) [set subgroup 01
                set color pink]
               if (cleavage-a = 0 and cleavage-b = 0) [set subgroup 00
                set color red]
               ]

   ;; turn prop-hard citizens into hardliners
   ;; and give them clustered locations that
   ;;depend on their cleavage-a group

   ask n-of round(prop-hard * n-pop) citizens
                  [set breed hardliners biased-scatter set shape
                   "person" set size 2]
   reset-ticks
end

to biased-scatter
         ;; hardliner positions are normally distributed with sd 5
         ;; around a mean of (+/-) hard-bias on each dimension
ifelse cleavage-a = 0
    [setxy random-normal hard-bias 5 random-normal hard-bias 5]
    [setxy random-normal (-1 * hard-bias) 5 random-normal (-1 * hard-bias) 5]
end
;;_____
;;
;; RUNTIME PROCEDURES
;;_____

to go
   ask citizens [
     set peer one-of other turtles
               ;; ALL CITIZENS choose random other AGENT as peer
               ;; NB voters mingle but hardliners can be peers

               ;; if both a and b categories the same, always interact
     if ([cleavage-a] of peer = [cleavage-a] of self and
         [cleavage-b] of peer = [cleavage-b] of self) [interact]

               ;; if peer is in the same category on a but not on b
               ;; interact with probability outgroup-openness
```

```
      if ([cleavage-a] of peer = [cleavage-a] of self and
          [cleavage-b] of peer != [cleavage-b] of self)
          [if (random-float 1 < outgroup-openness) [interact]]

                              ;; and vice versa
      if ([cleavage-a] of peer != [cleavage-a] of self and
          [cleavage-b] of peer = [cleavage-b] of self)
          [if (random-float 1 < outgroup-openness) [interact]]

                  ;; if peer is in the same category on neither a nor
                  ;; b, interact with probability outgroup-open-a ^ 2
      if ([cleavage-a] of peer != [cleavage-a] of self and
          [cleavage-b] of peer != [cleavage-b] of self)
          [if (random-float 1 < outgroup-openness ^ 2 ) [interact]]
      tick
  end

to interact
   set heading random-float 360
   forward reaction
              ;; first jump distance "reaction" in
              random direction
   face peer
              ;; then move towards peer by "attraction"
              ;; proportion of your distance from the
              peer
   forward distance peer * attraction
end

;;_____
;;
;; REPORTERS
;;_____

to-report dom-polarization
          ;; polarization of non- cross-cut subgroups
   let x00 mean [xcor] of turtles with [subgroup = 00]
          ;; normed by polarization of hardliners
   let y00 mean [ycor] of turtles with [subgroup = 00]
   let x11 mean [xcor] of turtles with [subgroup = 11]
   let y11 mean [ycor] of turtles with [subgroup = 11]
   let norm sqrt ((2 * hard-bias) ^ 2 + (2 * hard-bias) ^ 2)
   report sqrt ((x00 - x11) ^ 2 + (y00 - y11) ^ 2 ) / norm
end
```

```
to-report nondom-polarization
           ;; polarization of cross-cut subgroups
let x01 mean [xcor] of turtles with [subgroup = 01]
           ;; normed by polarization of hardliners
   let y01 mean [ycor] of turtles with [subgroup = 01]
   let x10 mean [xcor] of turtles with [subgroup = 10]
   let y10 mean [ycor] of turtles with [subgroup = 10]
   let norm sqrt ((2 * hard-bias) ^ 2 + (2 * hard-bias) ^ 2)
   report sqrt ((x01 - x10) ^ 2 + (y01 - y10) ^ 2 ) / norm
end
```

Appendix 4.2

XC Model Burn-in (Dominant Group Polarization Red, Nondominant Blue)[13]

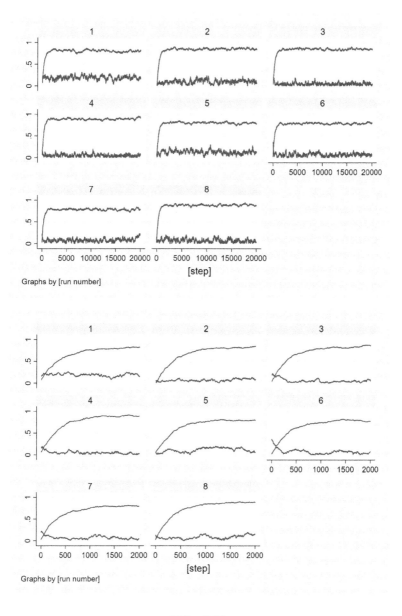

Graphs by [run number]

Graphs by [run number]

XC = 0.05

---

[13] The Behavior Space parameterization of these burn-in repetitions was:
["cleavage-a-mean" 0.5] ["cleavage-b-mean" 0.5] ["attraction" 0.1]
["hard-bias" 20] ["outgroup-openness" 0.05] ["prop-hard" 0.05]
["n-pop" 500] ["reaction" 2]
   ["xc" 0.05 (or 0.25, or 0.50)].

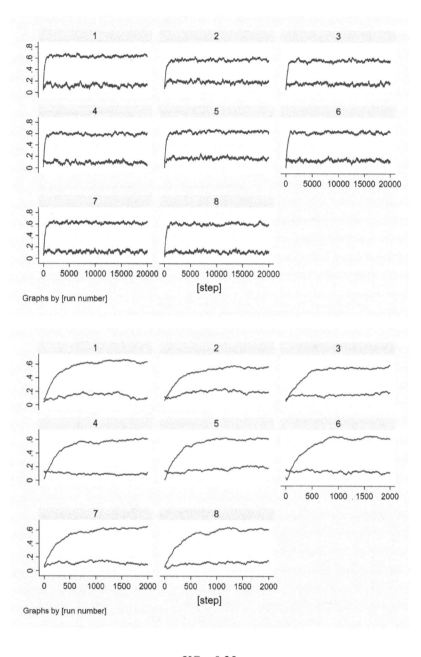

Graphs by [run number]

$$XC = 0.25$$

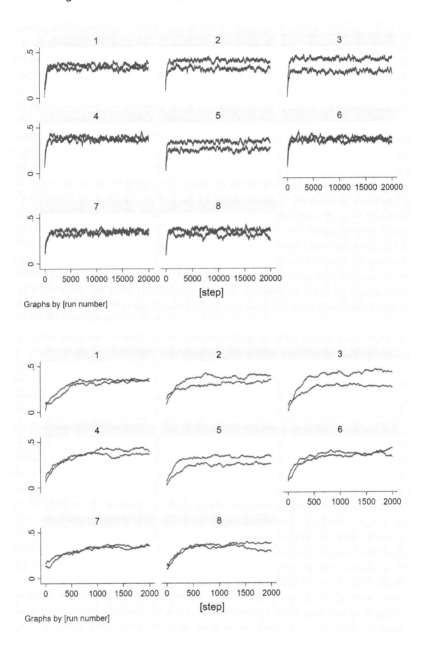

Graphs by [run number]

XC = 0.50

Appendix 5.1
Ethnocentrism 1.0, NetLogo code

```
turtles-own [ PTR cooperate-with-same? cooperate-with-different? ]
                                  ;; agents probability to reproduce
                                  ;; two key elements of strategy

to setup                          ;; create world with one agent per patch
    ca
    ask patches [ create-turtle ]
    reset-ticks
end

to create-turtle
    sprout 1 [

        set color random-color       ;; defined below

        set cooperate-with-same?
            (random-float 1.0 < immigrant-chance-cooperate-with-same)
                                  ;; probabilistically set strategy for
                                  ;; interacting with same color agent

        set cooperate-with-different?
            (random-float 1.0 < immigrant-chance-cooperate-with-different)
                                  ;; probabilistically set strategy for
                                  ;; interacting with different color agent

        update-shape             ;; agent's shape reflects its strategy

    ]
end

to-report random-color          ;; randomly choose one of these 4 colors
    report one-of [red blue yellow green]
end

to go
    immigrate
    ask turtles [ set PTR initial-PTR ]       ;; NB reset PTR to starting value
    ask turtles [ interact ]                  ;; all agents interact with others
    ask turtles [ reproduce ]                 ;; reproduce using post-
                                              ;; interaction PTR

    death                                     ;; kill some agents at random
                                              ;; NB NOT based on fitness (PTR)

    my-update-plots
    tick
end
```

```
to immigrate          ;; new agents enter the world on random empty cells
   let empty-patches patches with [not any? turtles-here]
   let how-many min list immigrants-per-day (count empty-patches)
                      ;; can't have more immigrants than empty patches
                      ;; how-many immigrants there are is the lesser of:
                      ;; immigrants-per-day, the number of empty patches
   ask n-of how-many empty-patches [ create-turtle ]
                      ;; "how-many" random empty patches create new agent
end

to interact
             ;; if I cooperate with agents of the same color, reduce my PTR by
             ;; cost-of-giving and increase PTR of neighbors by gain of receiving

   ask turtles-on neighbors4 [

     if color = [color] of myself
       [if [cooperate-with-same?] of myself [
         ask myself [ set PTR PTR - cost-of-giving ] ;; I pay
         set PTR PTR + gain-of-receiving]]         ;; neighbors gain

          ;; Note the nested "ifs". Payoffs only distributed above if my
          ;; neighbor is same color AND I cooperate with same; else zero.

          ;; Similarly, if we are different colors, if I cooperate with agents
          ;; of different color I reduce my PTR and reward my neighbors

     if color != [color] of myself [
       if [cooperate-with-different?] of myself [
         ask myself [ set PTR PTR - cost-of-giving ]
         set PTR PTR + gain-of-receiving]]
   ]
             ;; The net effect after all interactions is a PD game with the
             ;; mutual defection PTR payoff normalised to zero
end

to reproduce
             ;; use PTR to determine if the agent gets to reproduce
             ;; NB This is the replicator part of the replicator-mutator system
             ;; Agents use POST-INTERACTION PTR as probability they reproduce

   if random-float 1.0 < PTR [
     let destination one-of neighbors4 with [not any? turtles-here]
     if destination != nobody [
             ;; Agent can only reproduce if a von Neumann patch is empty
```

```
        hatch 1 [
                ;; Hatch a clone of the current turtle in the new location
            move-to destination
            mutate              ;; then mutate the clone/child
          ]
        ]
      ]
end
to mutate
                ;; modify the children of agents according to the mutation rate
                ;; NB This is the mutator part of the replicator-mutator system
                ;; children mutate according to the mutation rate

    if random-float 1.0 < mutation-rate [    ;; first mutate the color

      let old-color color
      while [color = old-color]
        [ set color random-color ]

                ;; MAKE the color change; NB not just give it a chance to change
    ]

                ;; now mutate the strategy variables, using NOT to toggle them

      if random-float 1.0 < mutation-rate [
        set cooperate-with-same? not cooperate-with-same?]
      if random-float 1.0 < mutation-rate [
        set cooperate-with-different? not cooperate-with-different?]

      update-shape          ;; the agent's shape reflects its strategy
end

to death      ;; kill each turtle with probability death-rate
    ask turtles [
      if random-float 1.0 < death-rate [ die ]
    ]
end

to update-shape         ;; make shape match strategy using nested
ifelse                  ;; agents cooperating with same are circles

      ifelse cooperate-with-same? [
        ifelse cooperate-with-different?
          [ set shape "circle" ]      ;; filled in circle (altruist)
          [ set shape "circle 2" ]    ;; empty circle (ethnocentric)

      ]

                ;; agents not cooperating with same are squares
      [
```

```
        ifelse cooperate-with-different?
            [ set shape "square" ]          ;; filled in square (cosmopolitan)
            [ set shape "square 2" ]        ;; empty square (egoist)
    ]
end

;;;;;;;;;
;;REPORTERS AND HOUSKEEPING
;;;;;;;;;

to-report cc_prop
    report count turtles with [shape = "circle"] / count turtles
end

to-report cd_prop
    report count turtles with [shape = "circle 2"] / count turtles
end

to-report dc_prop
    report count turtles with [shape = "square"] / count turtles
end

to-report dd_prop
    report count turtles with [shape = "square 2"] / count turtles
end

to my-update-plots                  ;; boilerplate plot management
    set-current-plot-pen "CC"       ;; altruists
    plotxy ticks count turtles with [shape = "circle"]
    set-current-plot-pen "CD"       ;; ethnocentric
    plotxy ticks count turtles with [shape = "circle 2"]
    set-current-plot-pen "DC"       ;; cosmopolitans
    plotxy ticks count turtles with [shape = "square"]
    set-current-plot-pen "DD"       ;; selfish
    plotxy ticks count turtles with [shape = "square 2"]
end

; Copyright 2003 Uri Wilensky. All rights reserved.
; The full copyright notice is in the Information tab.

; Pruned, edited and re-commented by Michael Laver
```

Cambridge Elements ☰

Quantitative and Computational Methods for the Social Sciences

R. Michael Alvarez
California Institute of Technology

R. Michael Alvarez has taught at the California Institute of Technology his entire career, focusing on elections, voting behavior, election technology, and research methodologies. He has written or edited a number of books (recently, *Computational Social Science: Discovery and Prediction*, and *Evaluating Elections: A Handbook of Methods and Standards*) and numerous academic articles and reports.

Nathaniel Beck
New York University

Nathaniel Beck is Professor of Politics at NYU (and Affiliated Faculty at the NYU Center for Data Science) where he has been since 2003; before which he was Professor of Political Science at the University of California, San Diego. He is the founding editor of the quarterly, *Political Analysis*. He is a fellow of both the American Academy of Arts and Sciences and the Society for Political Methodology.

About the Series

The Elements Series *Quantitative and Computational Methods for the Social Sciences* contains short introductions and hands-on tutorials to innovative methodologies. These are often so new that they have no textbook treatment or no detailed treatment on how the method is used in practice. Among emerging areas of interest for social scientists, the series presents machine learning methods, the use of new technologies for the collection of data and new techniques for assessing causality with experimental and quasi-experimental data.

Cambridge Elements $\equiv$

Quantitative and Computational Methods for the Social Sciences

Elements in the Series

Twitter as Data
Zachary Steinert-Threlkeld

A Practical Introduction to Regression Discontinuity Designs: Foundations
Matias D. Cattaneo, Nicolás Idrobo and Rocío Titiunik

Agent-Based Models of Social Life: Fundamentals
Michael Laver

Agent-Based Models of Polarization and Ethnocentrism
Michael Laver

A full series listing is available at: www.cambridge.org/QCMSS

CPSIA information can be obtained
at www.ICGtesting.com
Printed in the USA
LVHW080118180420
653724LV00003B/11

9 781108 796408